Aberdeenshire Library and Information Service
www.aberdeenshire.gov.uk/libraries
Renewals Hotline 01224 661511

HEADQUARTERS
- 8 FEB 2010
26 APR 2011
11 JUN 2011
- 2 JUL 2011

25 JUL 2014

HEADQUARTERS
17 MAR 2016
14 MAY 2016

22 OCT 2016
C 8 FEB 2017
12 APR 2018
30 APR 2018

ABERDEENSHIRE
LIBRARIES
WITHDRAWN
FROM LIBRARY

GEORGE, Tonia

Breakfast & brunch

D0344192

ALIS
2669199

breakfast & brunch

breakfast & brunch

delicious recipes to start the day

Tonia George

photography by Jonathan Gregson

RYLAND
PETERS
& SMALL

LONDON NEW YORK

Senior designer Megan Smith
Senior editor Céline Hughes
Production controller Ros Holmes
Art director Leslie Harrington
Publishing director Alison Starling

Food stylist Tonia George
Prop stylist Liz Belton
Assistant food stylist Siobhan Boyle
Indexer Hilary Bird

ABERDEENSHIRE LIBRARY AND	
INFORMATION SERVICES	
2669199	
HJ	2569606
641.52	£16.99
AD	ANF

First published in 2009 by
Ryland Peters & Small
20–21 Jockey's Fields
London WC1R 4BW
www.rylandpeters.com

10 9 8 7 6 5 4 3 2 1

Text © Tonia George 2009
Design and photographs
© Ryland Peters & Small 2009

ISBN: 978-1-84597-909-6

All rights reserved. No part of this
publication may be reproduced, stored
in a retrieval system or transmitted in
any form or by any means, electronic,
mechanical, photocopying or otherwise,
without the prior permission of the
publisher.

A CIP record for this book is available
from the British Library.

Printed and bound in China

Notes

• All spoon measurements are level,
unless otherwise specified.
• Ovens should be preheated to the
specified temperature. Recipes in this book
were tested using a regular oven. If using a
fan-assisted oven, follow the manufacturer's
instructions for adjusting temperatures.
• All eggs are medium, unless otherwise
specified. Recipes containing raw or partially
cooked egg, or raw fish or shellfish, should
not be served to the very young, very old,
anyone with a compromised immune
system or pregnant women.
• Sterilize preserving jars before use.
Wash them in hot, soapy water and rinse in
boiling water. Place in a large saucepan, then
cover with hot water. With the lid on, bring
the water to the boil and continue boiling
for 15 minutes. Turn off the heat, then leave
the jars in the hot water until just before
they are to be filled. Invert the jars onto
clean kitchen paper to dry. Sterilize the lids
for 5 minutes, by boiling, or according to
the manufacturer's instructions. Jars should
be filled and sealed while they are still hot.

Contents

Rise & shine!

Breakfast is by far and away my favourite meal of the day, which is ironic because mornings are probably my least favourite time of the day. Some days the thought of a frothy mocha and a slab of sourdough toast slathered in peanut butter is the only incentive there is to throw back the duvet and face the world.

And if it's difficult enough to force yourself out of bed, it's an even tougher job luring other grumpy heads out of their warm, cosy slumber. That must be why typical breakfast and brunch dishes are so full of vibrant flavours; salty bacon, sweet ambrosial maple syrup, creamy eggs, steaming coffee, voluptuous yoghurt and zingy fruits. I defy anyone to sleep on contentedly once the smoky aromas of bacon frying and toast turning golden creep up their nostrils.

Some days the thought of a frothy mocha and a slab of toast slathered in peanut butter is the only incentive there is to throw back the duvet and face the world.

Rushing out of the house with an empty tummy is never a good idea. Miss breakfast and research shows that you're more likely to suffer poor concentration and a slump in energy levels. Eating also kickstarts your metabolism and stabilizes blood sugar levels, so skipping a meal in the hope of saving on a few calories is counterproductive. Armed with the many recipes in this book, there really is no excuse. There are lots of quick ideas for rushed weekday mornings when everything seems to conspire against letting you leave the house on

time, from Nutty Honey Granola (page 33) and Rhubarb & Orange Compote (page 29), to a five-minute Banana, Honey & Wheatgerm Lassi (page 18) which can be wolfed down in a flash. Some you'll need to prepare on the weekend, but they promise to see you right through the week.

I have always been a huge fan of breakfast. When I was younger my mum made me toast before school every single morning — always one with Marmite and one with marmalade. If we were late for school the toast would be shimmied onto a piece of kitchen paper and I'd finish it in the car. But when the weekend came around it was a different story. The whole family wandered about in their dressing gowns in a well-rehearsed formation, each with their own job: the chief toast maker, someone to make the coffee, and another at the hob turning rashers of bacon and links of sausages until the table was groaning with food.

On birthdays and Mother's Day the mornings would stretch a little further, sometimes into the afternoon. After appetites had been whetted with Buck's Fizz, we would dig into bowls of Greek yoghurt scattered with pecans, drizzled with honey and topped with chunks of tropical fruit. After a short break we'd be back for Blueberry Pancakes (page 89), light and fluffy enough to absorb twice their weight of maple syrup, or sometimes a buttery Smoked Haddock Kedgeree (page 113) hiding lovely chunks of fresh fish and still-squidgy boiled egg.

It's very insightful to see how people start their days. There are those that go for the sugar and caffeine rush of a coffee and a pastry, others who need a plateful of eggs and

Breakfast stirs up cosy, nostalgic memories evoking hearth and home, and having someone cook it for you makes you feel nurtured.

sausages alongside mountains of toast, and plenty of others still that dare not deviate from their more virtuous bowl of oats. I've included recipes to please all of you, from hurried weekday breakfasts to leisurely weekend brunches. In fact a weekend brunch is a good chance to try some of the more eclectic dishes. After the repetitive rhythm of the week, it's a time when I like to explore what other cultures eat. In England we've been doing this since the Victorian times, when kedgeree was introduced to the breakfast table from India. Likewise, in California, Huevos Rancheros (page 49) has now become a staple brunch fixture. There are many other dishes that I have borrowed for this book, such as Spain's delicious cinnamon sugar-coated Churros (page 78), and the Scandinavian Gravadlax (page 119), to modern Australian classics such as Corn Cakes with Bacon & Avocado (page 106) born of a love for fresh ingredients.

Of course, I'm very particular about what goes on my breakfast plate, and I find that most people are. Eggs must be cooked to perfection – for me this means they need to ooze with an ocherous yolk but for others any trace of wobble will have been left far behind. My bacon needs to be so crisp that it snaps, but you might find it too dry like this. And whereas some balk at the marriage of sweet maple syrup with smoky bacon, I couldn't imagine life without it. So feel free to adapt the recipes to suit your own set of foibles; that's exactly what makes us who we are.

More than any other meal, I've also noticed how breakfast turns grown adults back into fussy children. Look at the way people cling to their favourite childhood cereal all through their adult life, and never lose the wide-eyed pleasure at seeing a stack of pancakes dripping with butter. Breakfast stirs up cosy, nostalgic memories evoking hearth and home, and

having someone cook it for you makes you feel nurtured. This is what makes it a special meal.

I also find brunching to be a rather intimate ritual. Sharing your morning meal tends to be reserved for partners and family and so brunch is where friendships are cemented and intimate secrets spilled. You might breakfast alone, but it's never okay to brunch alone. Perhaps this is the only real difference in breakfasting and brunching, because after all, when exactly does a breakfast become a brunch? Does it depend on what, when or how much you eat? Is anything more than three slices of toast after noon considered brunch? There is no definitive answer. The actual term was recorded by Guy Beringer in his visionary article 'Brunch: A plea' published in *Hunter's Weekly* in 1895. He makes a case for replacing the post-hunt meal with a multi-course feast starting with more breakfast-friendly fare. 'Brunch is cheerful, sociable and

compelling… and sweeps away the worries and cobwebs of the week', he wrote. It caught on in affluent social circles, but wasn't fully embraced until it crossed the Atlantic in the 1930s, where it took off as an indulgent Mother's Day treat.

Even now 'doing brunch' implies a certain amount of hedonism. Stretching the morning meal into the afternoon hours usually comes about after an eventful evening which has encroached upon your night of sleep. This is what feels so decadent about brunch. It defies convention and is full of contradictions: you can ignore alarm clocks, eat something sweet before your savoury course, enjoy cake before noon and have a cocktail alongside a boiled egg. It is truly a time when you can do what you want to rather than what you should do – a sentiment that very much appeals as I roll over, smile contentedly and switch off my bleeping alarm clock on a Saturday morning.

drinks

Carrot, apple & ginger juice Pear, kiwi & apple juice **Basil limeade**
Pineapple & mint agua fresca Pomegranate & orange sunrise **Banana,
honey & wheatgerm lassi** Cashew nut & mango smoothie Raspberry,
strawberry & orange juice **Bloody mary** Sea breeze Blood orange &
campari mimosa **Lemon & sage tisane** Real hot chocolate Spiced mocha

Carrot, apple & ginger juice

4 carrots
2 apples, quartered
3 cm fresh ginger
ice, to serve
a juicer
SERVES 2

There is something about this blend of fruit and vegetables that feels so extremely virtuous and cleansing. It is very thirst-quenching as well, especially when served really well chilled. Great for a hangover.

Pass the carrots, apples and ginger through a juicer, one at a time, into a jug. Add enough ice for 2 people and serve.

Pear, kiwi & apple juice

3 pears, quartered
3 kiwi fruit, quartered
1 apple, quartered
ice, to serve
a juicer
SERVES 2

Kiwis are my secret weapon against colds, being rich in vitamin C. They are sharp and sweet, and mixed with the mellower flavours of pears and apples they make a really gorgeous early-morning juice.

Pass the pears, kiwis and apples through a juicer, one at a time, into a jug. Add enough ice for 2 people and serve.

Basil limeade

225 ml freshly squeezed
    lime juice (from about
    10 limes)
75 g light muscovado sugar
20 g fresh basil leaves
2 handfuls of ice
250 ml soda water
*4–6 cocktail glasses, chilled
    in the freezer for 1 hour*
SERVES 4–6

If I'm having a brunch gathering then this basil limeade is what I serve to guests. The amount of lime and sugar is a personal thing, so I suggest you adjust it to taste, adding more of one or the other as necessary. There will be guests who will appreciate a cheeky dash of cachaça rum in theirs for a caipirinha-style cocktail.

Put the lime juice, sugar and basil in a blender (one that is able to crush ice) and blend until smooth. Add the ice and blend briefly to break up the ice cubes. Pour into the cocktail glasses and top up with the soda water.

Basil limeade (right)

Pineapple & mint agua fresca

100 g granulated sugar

a smallish pineapple (about 700 g), peeled and cored

a small handful of fresh mint leaves, plus extra to serve

ice, to serve

600 ml chilled soda water (optional)

SERVES 4–8

Refreshing *agua fresca* is found all over Mexico. The name literally means 'cold water' and it can be any fruit (or even another ingredient such as tamarind or rice and milk) blended with ice, sugar and water. The idea is that it is cooling and rehydrating on a hot day. Serve it as a whipped fruit frappé just with ice, or as a sparkling drink mixed with soda water.

Put the sugar and 100 ml water in a saucepan and heat gently until the sugar has dissolved. Remove from the heat and leave to cool while you cut the pineapple into rough chunks. Put the pineapple in a blender with the mint and the cooled syrup. Blend until smooth. Divide between 4 tumblers with a scoop of ice in each one, or 8 tall glasses and top up with ice and the soda water.

Pomegranate & orange sunrise

ice, to serve

500 ml freshly squeezed orange juice

200 ml pure pomegranate juice

SERVES 2

A twist on the usual tequila sunrise, mine is made with the newly fashionable pomegranate juice which adds a twist of bitterness to cut through the natural sweetness of orange juice. I sometimes add a shot of Campari to the pomegranate juice too, but this makes it an entirely different kind of morning!

Half fill 2 tumblers with ice and top up with orange juice so they are two-thirds full. Pour the pomegranate juice slowly down the side of the glass so it sinks to the bottom. Serve straightaway with a cocktail stirrer.

Banana, honey & wheatgerm lassi

2 bananas, peeled
2 teaspoons clear honey
100 g natural yoghurt
150 ml whole milk
1 tablespoon wheatgerm
    or wheat bran
SERVES 2

Some mornings I need a smoothie which is a meal in itself, especially if I am awake early and can't face eating. With the added bite of the wheatgerm, this lassi fits the bill. Lassi is a cooling Indian drink which can be sweet or savoury. In the summer I add a handful of ice before blending it for a more chilled drink. If you like ripe bananas, let the skins become speckled for a more intense experience.

Put the bananas, honey, yoghurt and milk in a blender and blend until smooth. Taste and add a little more honey if you think it needs it. Stir in the wheatgerm and blend briefly just to mix. Divide between 2 long glasses and serve with straws big enough for the wheatgerm not to cause blockages.

Cashew nut & mango smoothie

50 g shelled cashew nuts,
    soaked overnight in cold
    water
1 ripe mango, peeled and
    stoned
1 teaspoon linseed
SERVES 2

It's easy to forget how milky blended cashew nuts are, but they do make brilliant dairy-free smoothies. I like to blend mine with mango as it results in a super-thick smoothie verging on dessert territory. You could also use soft berries or bananas.

Drain the cashew nuts and put in a blender with 150 ml water. Blend until you have a smooth, nutty milk. Roughly chop the mango and add to the blender. Blend again, then stir in the linseed. Divide between 2 tumblers and serve.

Raspberry, strawberry & orange juice

125 g frozen raspberries
125 g strawberries, hulled
400 ml freshly squeezed
    orange juice
SERVES 2–4

I like to keep raspberries in my freezer for a rainy day as they add body to smoothies as well as a sharp burst of fruity flavour. There's no need to add ice, as the raspberries will make the drink lovely and icy for you.

Put the raspberries, strawberries and orange juice in a blender and blend until smooth. Divide between 2–4 tumblers and serve.

Raspberry, strawberry & orange juice; Banana, honey & wheatgerm lassi; and Cashew nut & mango smoothie (left to right)

Bloody mary

150 ml vodka

450 ml pure tomato juice

½ teaspoon hot
   horseradish sauce

1 teaspoon Worcestershire
   sauce

4 dashes Tabasco sauce

¼ teaspoon celery salt

½ teaspoon cracked black
   pepper

2 limes, cut into small
   wedges

ice, to serve

SERVES 4

There's nothing like a good Bloody Mary after a late night: it seems to get the blood pumping and cure any feelings of drowsiness. If you want a Virgin Mary leave out the vodka but squeeze in some more lime so you get more of a tang in it.

Mix all the ingredients together in a large jug. Taste and adjust the seasonings if necessary, adding more heat, pepper or lime as you wish. Add a couple of handfuls of ice and serve with a stack of tumblers.

Sea breeze

a handful of ice
150 ml pure pink grapefruit
  juice
300 ml pure cranberry juice
100 ml vodka
1 lime, cut into wedges
a cocktail shaker
SERVES 4

This is a great morning drink for summer. Simple to make and really refreshing but a few glasses will make you feel pleasantly sleepy, so watch you don't end up crawling back into bed.

Put the ice in the cocktail shaker along with the juices and vodka. Squeeze over a couple of lime wedges. Put the top on the shaker and shake a few times. Strain into 2 long glasses and add a lime wedge to each before serving.

Blood orange & campari mimosa

500 ml pure blood orange
  juice
2 tablespoons Campari
750-ml bottle sparkling
  white wine, chilled
SERVES 4

Mimosa or Buck's Fizz is a standard offering at brunch gatherings, but this one is different. The Campari and blood orange make it a little bitter, and this really whets the appetite. If anyone needs his or hers sweetened – not everyone gets the bitter thing – add a dash of agave syrup or honey and serve with a cocktail stirrer.

Divide the blood orange juice between 4 champagne flutes. Add a dash of Campari to each one, then top up with the wine.

Blood orange & campari mimosa (above)

Lemon & sage tisane

a small handful of fresh
    sage leaves
1 lemon
600 ml boiling water
1–2 teaspoons honey,
    to taste
SERVES 2

A tisane is a herbal tea, made strictly without real tea. Instead it is made by infusing herbs, spices or any aromatics in hot water. My lemony tisane infused with sage is a great drink for the morning – it will brighten your eyes and leave your face with a warm glow, if nothing else.

Put the sage leaves in a teapot. Using a potato peeler, pare off the lemon zest leaving behind the white pith underneath. Add this to the teapot. Halve the slightly naked-looking lemon and squeeze out all its juice, then set aside. Pour the boiling water over the leaves and zest and leave to steep for 3–5 minutes, depending on how strong you like it. Pour into 2 mugs and add lemon juice and honey to taste.

Real hot chocolate

500 ml whole milk
1 vanilla pod, split
    lengthways
75 g plain chocolate (at
    least 70% cocoa solids),
    coarsely grated, plus
    extra to dust
1 tablespoon light
    muscovado sugar
SERVES 2

Once you have had proper hot chocolate there is no going back I'm afraid. Pick a really good cooking chocolate with at least 70% cocoa solids to make this, so that you get a really chocolatey flavour.

Pour the milk into a saucepan and add the vanilla pod. Slowly bring to a gentle simmer, then remove from the heat and set aside for 10 minutes to allow the flavour to infuse the milk. Add the chocolate and sugar and whisk into the milk until melted and dissolved. Return to a low heat until steaming, but not boiling. Remove the vanilla pod, then divide between 2 mugs. Dust with chocolate.

Spiced mocha

300 ml whole milk
1 cinnamon stick
a pinch of grated nutmeg
2 shots of espresso coffee
2 tablespoons cocoa
    powder
1–2 tablespoons demerara
    sugar
100 ml whipping cream,
    whipped to soft peaks
SERVES 2

I find coffee to be quite bitter but I love hot chocolate, so for me, this is the best of both worlds: the hit of caffeine with the luxurious sweetness of a good steaming mug of cocoa. The spices give it a real complexity and stop it becoming sickly sweet. I can't justify the whipped cream on top, but I think it would be foolish to make it without.

Pour the milk into a saucepan and add the cinnamon and nutmeg. Slowly bring to a gentle simmer, then remove from the heat and set aside for 10 minutes to allow the flavours to infuse the milk. Meanwhile, pour the espresso shots into a heatproof jug. Stir in the cocoa powder and sugar until blended. Add the hot milk and whisk until all the ingredients are well blended. Return to the pan and reheat gently. Divide between 2 mugs and top with whipped cream.

fruit, grains & oats

Strawberries with pine nuts & greek yoghurt Melon salad in stem ginger syrup **Poached pears in jasmine tea syrup with cinnamon & dates** Rhubarb & orange compote Grilled pink grapefruit with vanilla sugar **Bircher muesli** Toasted coconut & tropical fruit muesli Nutty honey granola **Porridge with apples & blackberries** Deep coconut & sour cherry oaty bars Apricot & pumpkin seed granola bars **Irish oatmeal with bananas, maple syrup & pecans** Granola, nectarine & ricotta parfait

Strawberries with pine nuts & greek yoghurt

450 g strawberries,
hulled and halved

2 tablespoons golden
granulated sugar

3 tablespoons dark
muscovado sugar

250 g Greek yoghurt

25 g pine nuts

SERVES 4

When strawberries are at their most fragrant, with their candy floss perfume, this is the perfect breakfast dish to whip up. Crumbling dark muscovado sugar over the voluptuous Greek yoghurt creates a pool of fudginess on top. All the treacly flavours which come from the natural molasses in the sugar are drawn out; these contrast beautifully against the yoghurt and enhance the sweet berries.

Put the strawberries in a bowl and scatter over the granulated sugar. Cover and leave to macerate for 10 minutes. Scatter the muscovado over the yoghurt in a separate bowl and set aside. Meanwhile, put the pine nuts in a heavy-based frying pan over low heat and toast for 2–3 minutes, shaking them about until they become golden on all sides.

Divide the strawberries between 4 bowls. Swirl the now fudgy muscovado through the yoghurt and spoon on top of the strawberries. Scatter the pine nuts on top of the strawberries and serve.

Melon salad in stem ginger syrup

100 g light muscovado
sugar

50 g stem ginger, drained
and finely chopped

freshly squeezed juice of
1 lemon

1 charentais or Cantaloupe
melon, peeled and
deseeded

200 g raspberries
(optional)

SERVES 4

Ginger and melon are quite simply a match made in culinary heaven. The sweetness of one sets off the sharpness of the other one and vice versa. Make this when melons are bursting with ripe perfume and the raspberries, if you'd like to use some, are as sweet as can be.

Put the muscovado sugar in a saucepan with the ginger and 200 ml water. Heat gently until the sugar has completely dissolved, then turn up the heat and simmer for 5 minutes. Remove from the heat and add the lemon juice. Leave to cool.

Slice or chop the melon, place in a bowl and pour over the syrup. Tumble over the raspberries, if using, then serve.

Poached pears in jasmine tea syrup
with cinnamon & dates

200 ml boiling water

1 tablespoon jasmine tea leaves

2 cinnamon sticks

75 g clear honey

4 small pears, peeled, halved and cored

225 g Medjool dates, stoned and sliced

natural yoghurt or ricotta, to serve

SERVES 4

I love using tea leaves to imbue syrups with a delicate flavour. Jasmine tea is one of the most fragrant flavours, especially if you look out for the high-quality teas whose leaves are furled into long shapes.

Leave the boiling water to cool for a few minutes so it doesn't scorch the delicate tea leaves. Once it has cooled slightly – ideally 90°C, but don't worry, you don't need to check with a thermometer – you can pour it onto the jasmine tea leaves in a teapot or a heatproof jug. Leave it to steep for 3 minutes.

Strain the jasmine tea into a saucepan. Add the cinnamon and honey and place over medium heat. Bring it to a gentle simmer, then lower in the pears.

Cut out a disc of greaseproof paper to fit inside the pan, scrunch it up, then open it out again. Lower it into the pan and cover with the lid. Simmer gently for 8 minutes, then turn the pears so the other side sees the syrup (replacing the paper disc and lid). Simmer for 8 minutes. Add the dates and simmer for 5 minutes (still with the paper disc and lid on). Remove from the heat and leave to stand for 10 minutes. Serve warm or cold with natural yoghurt or ricotta.

Rhubarb & orange compote

400 g rhubarb (about
 6 sticks)
grated zest of ½ orange
freshly squeezed juice
 of 1 orange
1 vanilla pod, split
 lengthways
150 g light muscovado
 sugar
natural yoghurt or
 porridge, to serve

SERVES 4

Add blueberries or strawberries to this basic cushion of pink rhubarb. Keep your eye out for bright pink forced rhubarb, which is grown indoors in the dark for its lurid colour, making it an uplifting winter treat.

Preheat the oven to 180°C (350°F) Gas 4.

Trim the rhubarb to remove any leaves and the tough ends and cut into 7-cm lengths. Put these stubby bits of rhubarb, along with the orange zest, juice and vanilla pod in a large baking dish and scatter the sugar over the top. Cover the dish with aluminium foil and roast in the preheated oven for 15–20 minutes, until the rhubarb compliantly softens up.

Leave to cool and serve with a generous dollop of yoghurt or a bowl of steaming porridge, or simply by itself. Store in the fridge for up to 1 week.

Grilled pink grapefruit with vanilla sugar

2 pink grapefruits

1 vanilla pod, split lengthways

2 tablespoons golden caster sugar

natural yoghurt, to serve (optional)

SERVES 4

This is a quick and easy way to serve zingy grapefruit. If you happen to have one of those snazzy curved grapefruit knives, now is the moment you have been waiting for. You really do need to loosen the flesh from the shell before you grill it, as a hot grapefruit becomes quite dangerous when you try to delve into it with a spoon. Don't fret if you don't have a grapefruit knife – a small paring knife does a good job too.

Halve the grapefruits and slice a little off each top and bottom so they sit securely on a flat surface. Loosen the flesh from the shell with a curved grapefruit knife or small paring knife.

Scrape the seeds out of the vanilla pod and add to the sugar. Mix thoroughly with the back of a spoon to spread out the seeds.

Preheat the grill.

Place each grapefruit half on a baking tray and sprinkle the sugar over them. Slide under the grill and let the sugar melt and caramelize. It should only take 2–3 minutes. Remove from under the grill and leave to cool for 2 minutes. Serve with natural yoghurt on the side or if you are being abstemious, by itself.

Bircher muesli

125 g rolled oats

75 g golden sultanas

175 ml pure apple juice

freshly squeezed juice of 1 lemon

100 g natural yoghurt

1 apple, cored, peeled and grated

25 g flaked almonds

mixed summer berries, to serve

clear honey, to serve

SERVES 4–6

This is what I like to call summer porridge. It has the type of texture you either love or hate. I adore it – there is something comforting about its soggy sweetness – but my husband prefers crunchy granola. Each to his own. It will keep for 2–3 days in the fridge, but in that case, leave the apple out so it doesn't brown.

Put the oats and sultanas in a large dish. Pour over the apple and lemon juices. Cover with a tea towel and leave to soak overnight. Alternatively place everything in an airtight container and stick in the fridge, especially if it is very hot.

The next morning when you're ready for breakfast, stir the yoghurt, apple and almonds into the soaked muesli. Divide between 4–6 bowls, scatter some brightly coloured berries over the top and finish with a zigzag of clear honey.

Bircher muesli (right)

Toasted coconut & tropical fruit muesli

300 g rolled oats
50 g black (or white)
   sesame seeds
50 g sunflower seeds
125 ml pure apple juice
3 tablespoons vegetable oil
50 g desiccated coconut
50 g dried mango,
   finely chopped
50 g dried pineapple,
   finely chopped
50 g dried papaya,
   finely chopped
2 large baking trays, lined
   with baking parchment
SERVES 6–8

This toasted muesli is made with apple juice instead of being coated in sugar or honey, as most granola is. It crisps up the oats, but isn't overly sweet. I like the chewy tanginess of tropical fruits, but any dried fruits will work as they are simply stirred in at the end. If you can find some black sesame seeds, often sold in Asian grocers, they stand out more, but the regular ones are fine too.

Preheat the oven to 150°C (300°F) Gas 2.

Pour the oats and seeds into a really large mixing bowl, then stir in the apple juice and oil. Toss well until the juice has soaked into the dry ingredients. Tip half of the mixture onto each prepared baking tray and spread out evenly. Bake in the preheated oven for 25 minutes, until the oats are starting to toast.

Remove the trays from the oven and give everything a good stir. Add the desiccated coconut to the oat mixture and bake for a further 20 minutes. Leave to cool completely.

When the muesli is cold, stir in all the chopped dried fruit and toss to distribute evenly. Store in an airtight container and eat within 3 weeks.

Nutty honey granola

125 g maple syrup
125 g clear honey
4 tablespoons sunflower oil
250 g rolled oats
75 g shelled almonds,
   roughly chopped
75 g shelled Brazil nuts,
   roughly chopped
50 g pumpkin seeds
½ teaspoon salt
100 g golden sultanas
2 baking trays, lined with
   baking parchment
SERVES 10–12

Mmmm, crunchy honeyed granola. This version is very sweet and crunchy and quite rich so you don't need a lot. I tend to have a scattering with my yoghurt rather than the other way round. The trick is to get it to brown evenly, so you need it to be spread out and to turn it during roasting. Don't let it become too dark or it gets bitter. If in doubt, take it out and leave it to cool a little, then taste it and you can always put it back in for longer.

Preheat the oven to 140°C (275°F) Gas 1.

Put the maple syrup, honey and oil in a small saucepan and set over low heat to warm though. Put the oats, nuts, seeds and salt in a large mixing bowl and stir well. Pour over the warmed syrup and mix thoroughly with a wooden spoon. All the oats must be moistened.

Spread the granola over the prepared baking trays, making sure it is no deeper than 1 cm, and bake in the preheated oven for 20 minutes.

Remove the trays from the oven and stir the toasted, golden granola from the edges to the centre, then smooth out again. Return to the oven for a further 15–20 minutes, until lightly golden. Don't expect it to become crunchy – the mixture will remain soft until it cools.

Remove from the oven and leave to cool for 10 minutes before stirring in the sultanas. Leave to cool completely, then break into pieces. Store in an airtight container and eat within 1 month.

Nutty honey granola (left)

Porridge with apples & blackberries

100 g rolled oats

250 ml whole milk,
   plus a little extra to thin

a pinch of salt

75 g sultanas

1 tablespoon butter

2 apples, cored and cut
   into slim wedges

3 tablespoons demerara
   sugar

a pinch of ground
   cinnamon

100 g blackberries

SERVES 4

Everyone likes their porridge prepared differently. Personally I find porridge made with all milk too claggy and when it's made with just water a little insipid, unless you add a swirl of cream at the end which rather defeats the purpose of using good old water. A pinch of salt is a must too, as this stops it from being flabby and gives it some backbone.

Put the oats in a saucepan and add the milk and 250 ml water. Add a pinch of salt, cover with a lid and slowly bring to the boil over medium heat. Once the mixture is bubbling, turn the heat to low, add the sultanas and cook for 2–3 minutes, stirring occasionally. The porridge should be thick and creamy. Take off the heat and leave to stand with a lid on for 2–3 minutes while you cook the apples.

Put the butter in a frying pan over high heat until the bubbling subsides. Stir in the apples, sugar and cinnamon. Leave to caramelize for 2–3 minutes, then flip the apple wedges over so the other side gets a chance to become golden too. Finally, add the blackberries and heat for a couple of minutes just so they warm through a little.

Meanwhile, spoon the porridge into 4 bowls and stir in a little cold milk to stop it becoming too thick. Spoon the caramelized apples and blackberries on top and serve straightaway.

Deep coconut & sour cherry oaty bars

100 g dried sour cherries

100 g unsalted butter, cubed

125 g golden syrup

175 g light brown sugar

1/2 teaspoon ground cinnamon

75 g desiccated coconut

225 g rolled oats

75 g self-raising flour

1/2 teaspoon bicarbonate of soda

a pinch of salt

a 20 x 20-cm baking tin, lined with baking parchment

MAKES 9

These oaty bars flecked with dried cherries are chewy and moist; in fact they are on their way to becoming flapjacks. The butter and syrupy sweetness in them are usually reserved for an indulgent teatime treat, but they also go down very well in the morning.

Preheat the oven to 180°C (350°F) Gas 4.

Put the cherries in a bowl of boiling water and leave to soak for 10 minutes.

Meanwhile, put the butter, golden syrup and sugar in a saucepan and heat gently until dissolved and melted. Stir in the cinnamon. Pour the coconut, oats, flour, bicarbonate of soda and salt over the butter mixture and stir to combine. Drain the cherries and add those. Once everything is well mixed, pack the mixture into the prepared baking tin, pressing it down with a palette knife to compact it. Bake in the preheated oven for 25–30 minutes, until golden at the sides.

Remove from the oven and leave to cool for 10 minutes. Turn the mixture out onto a chopping board and cut into 9 squares. Leave to cool, then store in an airtight container and eat within 5 days.

Apricot & pumpkin seed granola bars

225 g rolled oats

100 g pumpkin seeds

50 g wheatgerm or wheat bran

1/2 teaspoon ground ginger

1/2 teaspoon salt

85 g dried apricots, chopped

150 g honey

50 g light muscovado sugar

6 tablespoons sunflower oil

a 20 x 30-cm baking tin, lined with baking parchment

MAKES 14

In the name of good health, I have come up with a crunchier, snappier, less buttery bar than those above. They are not chewy but they will hit the spot in the morning. You can vary the dried fruit and spice as much as you like as long as you stick to the basic premise.

Preheat the oven to 180°C (350°F) Gas 4.

Put the oats, pumpkin seeds, wheatgerm, ginger, salt and apricots in a large mixing bowl. Put the honey, sugar and oil in a saucepan over low heat. Heat for 4–5 minutes, until the sugar has melted into the butter.

Remove from the heat and pour the melted mixture over the dry ingredients in the mixing bowl, stirring so the mixture moistens all over. Spoon the mixture into the prepared baking tin and smooth it out with a palette knife. Bake in the preheated oven for 20–22 minutes, until golden around the edges.

Remove from the oven and leave to cool for 10 minutes. Turn the mixture out onto a chopping board and cut into 14 bars. Leave to cool, then store in an airtight container and eat within 5 days.

Apricot & pumpkin seed granola bars, and Deep coconut & sour cherry oaty bars (left to right)

Irish oatmeal with bananas, maple syrup & pecans

175 g Irish or steel-cut
   oats
a pinch of salt
50 g shelled pecan nuts,
   chopped
3 tablespoons double
   cream
2 bananas, sliced
maple syrup, to serve
SERVES 4–6

For proper oatmeal you will need to buy oats that haven't been rolled. These are called Irish, steel-cut or pinhead oats and are coarser than rolled oats. This means a lot of extra cooking, which in turn means you need to reorganize yourself and put the oats on before you feed your cats, shower etc., and then you won't have to wait for them. The result is a much more al dente mass of oaty nuggets in a creamy risotto-like sauce. They also need quite a generous pinch of salt.

Heat 1.2 litres water in a heavy-based saucepan until it comes to the boil, then tip in the oats and salt. Cover with a lid and turn the heat down as low as possible so there is no danger of catching.

Put the pecans in a dry frying pan over medium heat and leave them to heat up. Stir so they brown evenly, then remove from the heat and set aside.

Go off and have your shower or walk the dog and, after 30 minutes, the oats will be ready. Check they are not sticking after about 20 minutes, the first time you cook them. After that you will have it all sussed out.

Stir in the cream, then spoon into bowls and scatter over the bananas and pecans. Serve with maple syrup.

Granola, nectarine & ricotta parfait

150 g natural sheep's
   yoghurt
250 g ricotta
300 g Nutty Honey
   Granola (page 33)
4 nectarines, stoned
   and sliced
100 g raspberries
4 tablespoons clear honey,
   plus extra to drizzle
SERVES 4

These little pots of deliciousness are perfect to offer guests at a brunch party as an alternative to the fat-laden fry-up. Layer the ricotta, fruit and granola in glasses for a groovy look. You can vary the fruit depending on the season, but if you use hard fruits, such as apples or pears, poach them in some sugar syrup first until they are as soft as a ripe nectarine.

Put the yoghurt and ricotta in a bowl and beat together until combined.

Divide half the granola between 4 glasses, then put some nectarine slices and raspberries on top of that. Top with some of the yoghurt mixture and honey.

Top with the remaining granola, followed by more nectarines and raspberries, saving a few for the top, and another spoonful or two of the yoghurt mixture. Arrange the remaining fruit on top, drizzle with more honey and serve straightaway.

Granola, nectarine & ricotta parfait (right)

eggs

Eggs benedict Fried eggs with sage pangritata, asparagus & pancetta
Herb fritters with fried eggs & sumac tomatoes Poached eggs on
spinach with yoghurt & spiced butter Eggs en cocotte with leeks &
tapenade **Scrambled eggs with smoked trout & shiso** Huevos rancheros
Soft-boiled eggs with parma ham-wrapped focaccia **Caramelized chicory
with black forest ham & poached eggs** French toast with provolone
& semi-dried tomatoes Omelette with chives & gruyère **Smoked
haddock, radish & avocado omelette wraps** Tortilla with potatoes,
chillies & roasted pimentos Wild mushroom mini-frittatas with garlic
sourdough croutons

Eggs benedict

4 large eggs

4 wholemeal muffins,
  halved horizontally

8 slices of thin-cut ham

freshly ground black
  pepper

HOLLANDAISE SAUCE

2 tablespoons white wine
  vinegar

1 shallot, roughly chopped

½ teaspoon black
  peppercorns

2 large egg yolks

120 g unsalted butter

SERVES 4

This dish is all about timing. Get everything ready before you cook the eggs and you won't have to rush. Hollandaise sauce made in a blender is easy – just add the butter very slowly and you should hear the sauce turning thick and slushy.

Preheat the grill.

To make the hollandaise sauce, put the vinegar, 2 tablespoons cold water, the shallot and peppercorns in a saucepan and simmer over low heat for a few minutes until you have 1 tablespoon liquid remaining. Strain into a blender (or in a bowl if you are going to use an electric handheld whisk) with the egg yolks and set aside. Melt the butter in the same pan.

Fill a large, deep frying pan with water and bring to a demure simmer. Crack the eggs around the edge so they don't touch and poach for exactly 3 minutes.

Put the muffins (cut side up) and ham on a baking tray and grill for 2–3 minutes.

To finish the sauce, blend the eggs and vinegar until frothy. With the motor still running, add the melted butter in a very slow trickle until the sauce is thick. You should take about a minute to add all the butter. Any quicker and it will not emulsify and you'll be left with runny eggs.

Drape a slice of ham on top of each muffin half. Scoop out each poached egg and add to the stack. Pour over the hollandaise sauce and sprinkle with a grinding of black pepper.

Fried eggs with sage pangritata, asparagus & pancetta

40 g sourdough bread
  (about 2 slices), torn
  into chunks, crust and all

5 tablespoons olive oil

10 fresh sage leaves,
  shredded

400 g asparagus, trimmed

100 g pancetta, cubed

4 large eggs

sea salt and freshly ground
  black pepper

SERVES 4

Roasting asparagus is my favourite way of cooking it: the flavour is intensified and the ends get frazzled. Pangritata – fried breadcrumbs with herbs – was devised by the Italians to provide a similar texture and flavour to Parmesan, but cheaply.

Preheat the oven to 190°C (375°F) Gas 5.

Whizz the bread in a food processor until you get chunky, uneven crumbs. Tip out onto a baking tray and drizzle over 2 tablespoons of the oil, the sage and some seasoning. Toss everything together, then bake in the preheated oven for 15 minutes, stirring a couple of times to ensure it browns evenly.

Snap off the pale, woody ends of the asparagus and discard. Put the stems on a baking tray, drizzle with 2 tablespoons of the oil and season. Toss, then scatter

the pancetta over the top. Roast in the oven for 10–12 minutes, until the pancetta is cooked through and the asparagus is tender and slightly frazzled.

Heat the remaining oil in a frying pan over high heat, then crack an egg in each corner and turn the heat right down. Cook for 2–3 minutes until the white has set. If you need to firm up the white, cover with the lid for 30 seconds.

Divide the asparagus between 4 plates, top with an egg and sprinkle the pangritata over the top.

Eggs benedict (right)

Herb fritters with fried eggs & sumac tomatoes

200 g plum tomatoes,
  roughly chopped

2 teaspoons ground sumac

3 tablespoons extra virgin
  olive oil, or more

5 large eggs

1 teaspoon ground cumin

60 g fresh flat-leaf parsley,
  leaves roughly chopped
  and stalks discarded

20 g fresh coriander, leaves
  roughly chopped and
  stalks discarded

sea salt and freshly ground
  black pepper

SERVES 4

Sumac is a wild berry which, when dried and ground, adds a sour tang to food, a little like lemon juice. These herb fritters are a good way of using up leaves from a bush of herbs that needs trimming back. Serve it for a low-carb brekkie.

Preheat the oven to low.

Put the tomatoes and sumac in a bowl with 1 tablespoon of the oil. Season and toss until coated, then set aside.

Crack one of the eggs into a mixing bowl, season, add the cumin and beat to mix. Stir in the herbs. It will look like there is not enough egg, but you only need enough to bind it.

Heat a frying pan over high heat and add 1 tablespoon of the oil. Drop 2 tablespoons of the herb mixture in the pan to make your first fritter and continue until you run out of space in the pan.

Cook over high heat for 2 minutes on each side, until lightly golden. Keep warm in the oven while you fry the rest.

Once all the fritters are done, add the remaining oil to the same frying pan and wait for it to heat up. Crack the remaining eggs into the pan and fry for 2 minutes. Cover with a lid and cook for a further 30–40 seconds just to cook the top of the whites; you want the egg yolk to remain runny.

Divide the fritters between 4 plates, top with a fried egg and scatter the sumac tomatoes over the top.

Poached eggs on spinach with yoghurt & spiced butter

1 small garlic clove, crushed

200 g Greek yoghurt

50 g butter

$\frac{1}{2}$ teaspoon cumin seeds

$\frac{1}{2}$ teaspoon dried chilli
  flakes

$\frac{1}{2}$ teaspoon sea salt flakes

1 loaf of Turkish flat bread,
  cut into 4 squares and
  halved horizontally

1 tablespoon olive oil

400 g spinach

8 large eggs

sea salt and freshly ground
  black pepper

SERVES 4

This egg dish is popular in Australia where there is a big Turkish community. It is a great dish packed with so much flavour that you will be hooked from the first taste. If you can't get hold of Turkish bread then pita or sourdough work well.

Preheat the grill to high. Get everything ready before you start cooking: mix the garlic and yoghurt. Put the butter, cumin, chilli flakes and salt flakes in a small saucepan. Put the flat bread on a baking tray. Fill 2 deep frying pans with water and bring to the boil over high heat.

Heat a wok, then add the oil and when hot, add the spinach in batches. Toss around the wok so it cooks evenly and when it is just wilted, take it off the heat, season and cover.

Reduce the heat under the 2 frying pans to low so the water is barely simmering and break 4 eggs, far apart, into each pan. Leave for 3 minutes. Grill the bread, cut side up, until lightly toasted, then transfer to 4 plates. Spread some garlic yoghurt over the bread and heap a mound of spinach on top. Using a slotted spoon, sit a poached egg on top of each square of yoghurty bread. Quickly heat the spiced butter over high heat until bubbling, pour over the eggs and serve.

Poached eggs on spinach with yoghurt & spiced butter (left)

Eggs en cocotte with leeks & tapenade

25 g butter

2 leeks, thinly sliced

a pinch of ground nutmeg

2 tablespoons tapenade
(olive paste)

4 large eggs

2 tablespoons double
cream

sea salt and freshly ground
black pepper

granary toast or green
salad, to serve

4 x 150-ml ramekins

SERVES 4

Eggs *en cocotte* – baked eggs – are all about timing: you want that yolk to have a good molten ooze. Don't skip the *bain marie* part otherwise the whites will become overheated and tough. If you like you can put some chopped sautéed mushrooms or pesto in the base of the ramekins. Sometimes I buy porcini and truffle paste from a deli and use that, as it has such a natural affinity with eggs.

Preheat the oven to 200°C (400°F) Gas 6.

Heat the butter in a frying pan, add the leeks and cook gently for 5–6 minutes until soft. Season to taste with salt, pepper and nutmeg.

Spoon an equal amount of tapenade into each ramekin, then top with the leeks. Break an egg into each ramekin, season them too, then drizzle a trickle of the cream over the top of each.

Put the ramekins in a deep roasting tray in the oven and pour enough boiling water directly from the kettle into the roasting tray so that it comes about halfway up the sides of the ramekins. This is the *bain marie*. Bake in the preheated oven for 10–14 minutes – 10 minutes if you like the yolks to remain runny, and a few minutes more if you prefer them set.

Lift the ramekins carefully out of the roasting tray using tongs or a tea towel and serve straightaway as they will continue to cook. Serve with granary toast or green salad on the side.

Scrambled eggs with smoked trout & shiso

10 large eggs

4 tablespoons whole milk

50 g butter

4 slices of white bread

280 g hot smoked trout,
flaked

a handful of shiso cress

a pinch of Japanese chilli
pepper or chilli powder

sea salt and freshly ground
black pepper

SERVES 4

Scrambled eggs need to be cooked with patience to become creamy. If they are cooked properly, you will not have to resort to adding cream, which just hides an underlying bad scramble. Smoked trout goes exceedingly well with scrambled eggs and the pretty purple leaves of shiso cress decorate it and add a spicy kick.

Break the eggs into a mixing bowl and beat together with the milk and some salt and pepper.

Meanwhile, heat half the butter in a heavy-based saucepan over low heat until the bubbling subsides. Pour in the eggs and heat through, stirring occasionally, for 4–5 minutes, until they start to feel like they are in danger of catching on the base of the pan. Reduce the heat to its lowest setting and stir constantly for 3–5 minutes to make sure the eggs are not over-heating on the bottom of the pan.

Meanwhile, toast and butter the bread with the remaining butter. Take the eggs off the heat while they still look a little runny, add the trout, give them a final few stirs and divide between the pieces of toast. Scatter the shiso and a little chilli pepper over the top.

Scrambled eggs with smoked trout & shiso (right)

Huevos rancheros

3 tablespoons vegetable oil

1 green chilli, chopped

2 garlic cloves, crushed

500 g tomatoes, cut into
   slim wedges

400-g tin pinto or
   cannellini beans

50 g Cheddar, grated

freshly squeezed juice of
   1 lime, plus extra lime
   wedges to serve

a handful of fresh coriander
   leaves, chopped

4 eggs

4 corn tortillas

sea salt and freshly ground
   black pepper

SERVES 4

All over the States there are numerous versions of these 'ranch eggs'. I like to cook my salsa with fresh tomatoes and then serve it with mashed, cheesy beans. You can buy tins of refried beans but it is just as easy to mash your own. If you want to serve it with a spoonful of guacamole or soured cream, that's a great idea.

Heat 1 tablespoon of the oil in a large frying pan over medium heat, then add the chilli, half the garlic and a pinch of salt and fry for 1–2 minutes, until softened. Add the tomatoes and cook gently for about 20 minutes.

Heat the remaining oil in a small saucepan, add the remaining garlic and heat through for 20 seconds, until just browning. Add the beans, then using a potato masher, coarsely mash the beans and stir in plenty of salt and pepper and the Cheddar.

Stir the lime juice and coriander into the tomato sauce. Make 4 holes in the sauce and crack an egg into each one. Cook for 3 minutes until set. Cover with the lid for the last 30 seconds just to firm up the whites.

Meanwhile, heat a frying pan over medium heat. Cook the tortillas for 1 minute on each side, until golden and hot. Transfer to 4 plates and spread the beans over the tortillas. Top with tomato salsa and the eggs. Serve with lime wedges and guacamole or soured cream if you like.

Soft-boiled eggs with parma ham-wrapped focaccia

1 teaspoon anchovy paste

3 tablespoons extra virgin
   olive oil

8 x 1-cm slices of
   rosemary focaccia,
   halved horizontally

4 large eggs, at room
   temperature

8 slices of Parma ham,
   each torn in half

SERVES 4

The method below is by far the best for soft-boiling eggs. In fact, the word 'boiled' is misleading because boiling an egg toughens up the white, making it rubbery, not creamy. The timings here will give you a perfectly runny yolk with a set, creamy white. This will only work if the eggs are at room temperature to start with – don't cook them straight out of the fridge otherwise they will crack.

Preheat the grill.

Mix the anchovy paste with the oil and spread it over the focaccia. Bring a medium saucepan of water to a rolling boil. Lower in the eggs and turn the heat down so they simmer gently for 1 minute. Turn off the heat completely, cover with a lid and set your timer for 4 minutes.

Meanwhile, grill the focaccia, anchovy side up, for 1–2 minutes. Remove from under the grill and wrap a piece of Parma ham around each toast. Place on a plate with an egg cup. Remove the eggs from the water with a slotted spoon and transfer to the egg cups. Eat immediately otherwise the eggs will continue to cook.

Huevos rancheros (left)

Caramelized chicory with black forest ham & poached eggs

25 g butter

4 chicory heads,
   halved lengthways

4 eggs

100 g rocket

8 slices of Black Forest ham

25 g Parmesan, shaved

sea salt and freshly ground
   black pepper

DRESSING

1 small garlic clove,
   finely chopped

1 red chilli, finely chopped

1 tablespoon red wine
   vinegar

2 tablespoons extra virgin
   olive oil

finely grated zest and juice
   of ½ unwaxed lemon

SERVES 4

Chicory is such an underrated vegetable, unlike in France and Italy where they use it a lot, and not just in the salad bowl. It is so different when cooked, becoming silky smooth and slightly bitter, which is why it works so well against a sweet, smoky ham like Black Forest ham. The chilli and lemon in the dressing wake up all the flavours. If you make this once you'll be addicted.

Preheat the oven to low.

To make the dressing, put the garlic, chilli and vinegar in a bowl and whisk in the olive oil and lemon zest and juice.

Heat the butter in a large frying pan over low heat and add the chicory, cut side down. Season with salt and pepper, cover with a lid and leave the chicory to cook gently for 5–6 minutes. Remove the lid, turn up the heat and continue to cook for 5 minutes, until the chicory is golden. Turn the chicory halves over and cook for 3–4 minutes so the other side gets a chance to caramelize. Transfer to the oven to keep warm.

Fill a large, deep frying pan with water and bring to a demure simmer. Crack the eggs around the edge so they don't touch and poach for exactly 3 minutes.

Place a little mound of rocket on each plate, top with 2 chicory halves and drape the Black Forest ham on top. Scoop out each poached egg and place on top of the ham. Scatter some Parmesan shavings around the plate and finish with a drizzle of dressing.

French toast with provolone & semi-dried tomatoes

4 eggs

175 ml whole milk

4 x 3-cm slices of challah

1 tablespoon pesto

100 g Provolone or
   mozzarella, thinly sliced

6 semi-dried tomatoes,
   chopped

a handful of fresh basil
   leaves

2 tablespoons olive oil

sea salt and freshly ground
   black pepper

SERVES 4

French toast works really well as a savoury dish, too. This one is not dissimilar to the Italian *mozzarella in carrozza*, where a mozzarella sandwich dipped in egg is fried. You can vary the filling, adding ham or salami if you like. The important thing is that you soak the bread so it absorbs all the egg and finish it off in the oven after frying as it won't cook all the way through like a thin French toast.

Preheat the oven to 180°C (350°F) Gas 4.

Put the eggs and milk in a bowl and whisk together with a little salt and pepper. Using a paring knife, make a pocket in each slice of challah by cutting horizontally into the centre of one of the long sides. Spread a quarter of the pesto on the inside of each pocket, then fill with the provolone, tomatoes and basil. Place in a shallow dish, pour in the egg mixture and set aside for 10 minutes.

Heat the oil in a frying pan over high heat and fry the bread for 1–2 minutes on each side, until golden. Transfer to a baking tray and bake in the preheated oven for 10 minutes, until puffed up.

Caramelized chicory with black forest ham & poached eggs (right)

Omelette with chives & gruyère

3 eggs

2 tablespoons snipped
fresh chives

1 tablespoon butter

25 g Gruyère, grated

1 tablespoon double cream

sea salt and freshly ground
black pepper

a 20-cm frying pan

SERVES 1

A perfectly crumpled, soft omelette oozing with cheese is bliss. Too many omelettes are cooked badly, but once you master the technique, there's no end of combinations you can make. I love this indulgent filling, which complements, as opposed to overpowering the egg element of the omelette.

Gently beat the eggs in a bowl and season with salt and pepper. Stir in half the chives.

Heat the frying pan over high heat until really hot. Add the butter, wait for it to sizzle, then just as it wants to brown pour in the eggs. Leave them to become nicely golden on the outside – no more than 45 seconds – drawing the cooked edges into the centre. Tilt the pan so the

uncooked egg runs into the edges. When the omelette is evenly set, except for a little unset egg, it is done.

Remove the pan from the heat and add the Gruyère and cream in the centre. Fold 2 edges of the omelette over, then tilt the pan so you can slide it out and upturn it onto a plate, seam side down. Grind some pepper over the top and finish with the remaining chives.

Smoked haddock, radish & avocado omelette wraps

6 eggs

about 2 tablespoons butter

200 g hot smoked haddock,
flaked

50 g watercress

1 ripe avocado, peeled,
stoned and chopped

6 radishes, thinly sliced

2 tablespoons extra virgin
olive oil

2 tablespoons freshly
squeezed lemon juice

sea salt and freshly ground
black pepper

a 15–18-cm frying pan

SERVES 4

These wraps are a cross between a pancake and an omelette. You can use any smoked fish for this, but I like hot smoked fish as this dispenses with cooking it first. Salmon, mackerel and eel would all work just as well as the haddock I've used here. Make sure the avocado is soft and ripe and season it really well.

Preheat the oven to low.

Gently beat the eggs in a bowl and season with salt and pepper. Put an ovenproof plate in the oven to heat up.

Heat about 1 teaspoon of the butter in the frying pan over high heat and swirl it around the pan. Pour in about 3 tablespoons of the beaten eggs – just enough to coat the base of the pan. Wait for 30 seconds, then flip over. Repeat with the remaining mixture, using the same amount of butter each time,

until you have about 8 omelettes, keeping them warm on the plate in the oven.

Meanwhile, place the smoked haddock, watercress, avocado and radishes in a large mixing bowl. Stir in the oil and lemon juice and season with pepper.

Lay 2 omelettes out on a board and spoon some of the haddock filling down the middle of each one, then roll up and transfer to a plate. Repeat with the remaining wraps and 3 more plates.

Smoked haddock, radish & avocado omelette wraps (left)

Tortilla with potatoes, chillies & roasted pimentos

6 tablespoons olive oil

600 g (about 4) potatoes, peeled and thinly sliced

2 red chillies, thinly sliced

1 onion, thinly sliced

½ teaspoon sea salt

8 eggs

125 g marinated roasted pimentos, drained and sliced

a 20-cm non-stick frying pan, at least 7 cm deep

SERVES 6

The secret of a good tortilla is to soften the potatoes in lots of olive oil and then add them to the eggs and back into the pan, not the other way around. If you pour the eggs directly over the potatoes in the pan, they will not coat the potatoes evenly and you will get air bubbles. Don't rush the cooking either – the egg proteins will get agitated, resulting in a tough texture rather than a creamy finish.

Heat 4 tablespoons of the oil in the frying pan, then add the potatoes, chillies, onion and salt. Reduce the heat to low and cover with a lid. Cook for 15 minutes, stirring occasionally so the onions don't catch on the base of the pan.

Preheat the grill.

Beat the eggs in a large mixing bowl. Transfer the cooked ingredients from the frying pan to the beaten eggs and stir. Add the roasted pimentos.

Turn the heat up to medium under the frying pan and add the remaining oil. Pour the egg mixture into the pan. Cook for 4–5 minutes until the base is golden – loosen the sides and lift up to check.

Grill for 3–4 minutes, until it is cooked all the way through. Cut into wedges.

Wild mushroom mini-frittatas with garlic sourdough croutons

50 g Parmesan, grated,
plus extra for dusting

25 g dried porcini
mushrooms

25 g butter

3 shallots, finely chopped

2 garlic cloves, crushed

300 g wild mushrooms,
such as chanterelles
and trompettes

leaves from 2 sprigs of
fresh thyme

8 eggs

sea salt and freshly ground
black pepper

watercress, to serve

CROUTONS

2 slices of sourdough, torn
into 2-cm chunks, crust
and all

4 tablespoons olive oil

1 garlic clove, crushed

*a 9-hole muffin tin with
large (175-ml) holes*

MAKES 9

Frittatas look so cute when they are baked in individual muffin moulds. Make this at the end of the summer when wild mushrooms are cheap and plentiful. The sourdough croutons add a good contrast in texture.

Preheat the oven to 190°C (375°F) Gas 5. Grease the muffin tin and dust with Parmesan. Put the porcini in a little bowl with 2 tablespoons boiling water and leave to soak for 15 minutes.

To make the croutons, put the sourdough on a roasting tray, toss with the oil, garlic and seasoning and roast in the preheated oven for 20 minutes.

Melt the butter in a frying pan, then add the shallots and sauté over low heat for 5–6 minutes, until softened. Add the garlic and wild mushrooms, turn up the heat and cook for 3–4 minutes, until they become tender and any moisture has evaporated. Season well and add the thyme. Gently beat the eggs in a mixing bowl. Drain the soaked porcini and add to the eggs with the cooked ingredients from the pan, the Parmesan and some seasoning and beat. Divide between the muffin tin holes, dust with more Parmesan and cook in the preheated oven for 18–20 minutes, until just set.

Leave to stand for 5 minutes, then serve with watercress and the croutons.

pastries & bakes

Walnut bread with goats' cheese, honey & wet walnuts Easy sourdough bread **Chilli & cheddar cornbread** Lemon & sultana soda bread Banana & chocolate chip loaf **Marmalade & almond loaf** Crumpets Poppyseed bagels **Sticky cinnamon & cardamom palmiers** Jam & frangipane brioches Dairy-free banana, date & bran muffins **Exploding berry crumble muffins** Sugary jam doughnut muffins Chocolate chip & peanut butter muffins **Brioche french toast with pineapple & syrup** Apple streusel coffee cake Pecan & maple syrup sticky buns **Churros with cinnamon sugar** Apple turnovers

Walnut bread with goats' cheese, honey & wet walnuts

75 g clear honey,
    plus extra to serve

7 g dried active yeast

500 ml hand-hot water

100 g butter, melted

4 tablespoons walnut oil

200 g shelled dried
    walnuts, chopped

1 tablespoon sea salt

750 g wholemeal bread
    flour, plus extra for
    dusting

400 g fresh goats' cheese,
    to serve

a handful of wet (fresh)
    walnuts, or dried,
    to serve

2 baking trays,
    dusted with flour

MAKES 2 X 450-G LOAVES

In autumn when wet (fresh) walnuts abound, this is the most delicious way to serve them. The bread is quite sweet so it makes a lovely breakfast treat with chalky fresh goats' cheese and a bowl of wet walnuts. I like to serve these in their shells, which forces people to interact with the food and heightens the enjoyment.

Put the honey, yeast and water in a large bowl. Set aside in a draught-free place for 15 minutes until foamy on the surface. Pour in the butter, oil, walnuts and salt.

Place the flour in a food mixer with a dough hook attachment. Alternatively, do this by hand. Set the mixer to the lowest speed and stir in the foamy mixture. The dough should be soft and slightly sticky. Turn the mixer up (or use elbow grease!) and knead the dough for 10–15 minutes. Place in a clean, lightly oiled bowl, cover with clingfilm and leave in a warm place for 1 hour, or until it has doubled in size.

Gently push the air out of the dough and take it out of the bowl, keeping the top as untouched as possible as this will be the structure of your crust. Slice the

dough in half, shape into ovals and smooth the edges by drawing the rough edges underneath and pinching them together on the underside. The top should be smooth and slightly stretched. Transfer to the prepared baking trays, cover with a tea towel and prove for 20–30 minutes, until doubled in size. Preheat the oven to 230°C (450°F) Gas 8.

Dust the bread generously with flour and score the top with diagonal lines. Sprinkle the sides of the oven with a little water. Bake the bread in the preheated oven for 5 minutes, then reduce the heat to 200°C (400°F) Gas 6 and bake for a further 25–30 minutes, until golden brown and hollow-sounding when tapped underneath. Leave to cool on a wire rack.

Easy sourdough bread

400 g rye flour

2 teaspoons sea salt

200 ml hand-hot water

20 g fresh yeast or 10 g
   dried active yeast

250 g strong wholemeal
   bread flour

250 g strong white plain
   flour, plus extra for
   dusting

2 baking trays,
   dusted with flour

MAKES 2 X 450-G LOAVES

Real sourdough takes several days of commitment; as in the method below, you make a starter from flour and water and leave it until it begins to ferment and give off a tangy, alcoholic aroma. However, from here, you have to feed the starter to encourage the yeast to multiply. I have skipped this stage and just added the starter to the bread dough so that you get the tangy flavour without the wait.

To make the starter, put 150 g of the rye flour, the salt and water in a large bowl. Cover with clingfilm and leave at room temperature for 36 hours, by which time it should smell slightly tangy.

When you are ready to start making the dough, blend the yeast with 200 ml hand-hot water (crumble it in if it is fresh yeast or sprinkle if it is dried). Transfer the remaining rye flour, and the wholemeal and white flours to a food mixer with a dough hook attachment. Alternatively, do this by hand. Set the mixer to the lowest speed and stir in the yeast mixture, followed by the sourdough starter, adding a little more warm water if it is still dry to achieve a soft, slightly sticky dough.

Turn the mixer up (or use some elbow grease!) and knead the dough for 10–15 minutes. Place in a clean, lightly oiled bowl, cover with clingfilm and leave in a warm place for 1–2 hours, until it has almost doubled in size.

Gently push the air out of the dough and take it out of the bowl, keeping the top as untouched as possible as this will be the structure of your crust. Slice the dough in half and smooth the edges by drawing the rough edges underneath and pinching them together on the underside. The top should be smooth and slightly stretched, and the loaf round. Transfer to the prepared baking trays, cover with a tea towel and prove for 1 hour, until doubled in size. Meanwhile, preheat the oven to 230°C (450°F) Gas 8.

Dust the bread generously with flour and score the top with a criss-cross pattern. Sprinkle the sides of the oven with a little water. Bake the bread in the preheated oven for 5 minutes, then reduce the heat to 200°C (400°F) Gas 6 and bake for a further 25–30 minutes, until golden brown and hollow-sounding when tapped underneath. Leave to cool on a wire rack.

Chilli & cheddar cornbread

150 g plain flour

2 teaspoons bicarbonate
of soda

1 teaspoon sea salt

150 g medium cornmeal
or polenta

25 g caster sugar

2 green chillies, chopped

150 g Cheddar, grated

275 ml buttermilk

50 g butter, melted

1 egg, beaten

*a 22-cm round or 20-cm
square cake tin, greased*

SERVES 6–8

Cornbread is not really a bread at all but a crumbly, buttery cake which can be served with fried chicken, or buttered and eaten for breakfast with a strong black coffee. It makes a nice change next to a plate of baked beans too, especially if they're home-made, such as the ones on page 128.

Preheat the oven to 190°C (375°F) Gas 5.

Sift the flour and bicarbonate of soda into a mixing bowl and stir in the salt, cornmeal, sugar, chillies and Cheddar.

In another bowl, beat together the buttermilk, butter and egg. Pour into the dry ingredients and briefly fold in until no floury pockets remain. Scrape into the prepared cake tin and bake in the preheated oven for 20–25 minutes, until a skewer inserted into the centre comes out clean. Leave to cool in the tin for 5 minutes, then turn out onto a wire rack to cool completely.

Lemon & sultana soda bread

150 g sultanas

400 g wholemeal flour,
plus extra for dusting

2 teaspoons bicarbonate
of soda

2 tablespoons sugar

1 teaspoon sea salt

250 ml buttermilk

finely grated zest of
1 unwaxed lemon

a baking tray, lightly floured

a 22-cm round cake tin

SERVES 6–8

This soda bread is studded with sultanas and streaked with lemon zest, making it even more delicious than plain soda bread. It is one of the easiest breads to make because it requires no yeast, using bicarbonate of soda as a raising agent. I like to toast it, slather it with butter and eat it with one of the preserves in the last chapter of this book.

Preheat the oven to 220°C (425°F) Gas 7.

Soak the sultanas in 200 ml water for 15 minutes.

Put the flour, bicarbonate of soda, sugar and salt in a large mixing bowl. Make a well in the centre and pour in the buttermilk, sultanas and their water, gradually drawing in the floury mixture with a wooden spoon until you have a soft, slightly loose but not sticky dough.

Bring the dough together with your hands and shape into a round roughly 22 cm across and 5 cm deep. Don't knead the dough or overwork it as you would with a yeasted bread – use a light touch as you would when making scones.

Place on the prepared baking tray and score a large cross across the surface of the bread with a sharp knife. Dust with flour. Place the cake tin, upturned, on top of the bread to prevent it from browning too much. Bake in the preheated oven for 15 minutes. Reduce the heat to 200°C (400°F) Gas 6, remove the cake tin from on top of the bread and bake for a further 10–15 minutes, until it is hollow-sounding when tapped underneath. Leave to cool on a wire rack.

Chilli & cheddar cornbread (right)

Banana & chocolate chip loaf

225 g plain flour

1 teaspoon baking powder

½ teaspoon salt

175 g light muscovado
  sugar

400 g (about 4) over-ripe
  bananas, mashed

85 g butter, melted

2 large eggs, lightly beaten

100 g plain chocolate,
  roughly chopped

*a 900-g loaf tin, greased and
  base-lined with baking
  parchment*

SERVES 8–10

This is a cake that can't go wrong, unless you are not patient enough to wait for the bananas to ripen. This is a real no-no; they have to be black to get that deep flavour. In fact, in our house, we make this loaf to suit the look of our bananas, not the other way round. Saying that, we seem to let them go black a lot more than we need to, in anticipation of this cake. The chocolate chips are just gilding the lily but when they come out molten and oozy it makes the loaf irresistible.

Preheat the oven to 180°C (350°F) Gas 4.

Put the flour, baking powder and salt in a mixing bowl. In another bowl, mix the sugar and bananas until there are no large lumps. Beat in the butter and eggs.

Tip the wet ingredients into the dry ingredients and mix, being careful not to overmix otherwise the loaf will be tough. Stir in the chocolate. Spoon the thick batter into the prepared loaf tin and bake on the centre shelf of the preheated oven for 40–45 minutes, until a skewer inserted into the centre comes out clean.

Leave the loaf to cool in the tin for 10 minutes, then turn out onto a wire rack to cool completely. When cold, serve in slices with butter or a decadent dollop of ricotta.

Marmalade & almond loaf

225 g butter, softened

150 g golden caster sugar

freshly squeezed juice of
½ orange

finely grated zest of
1 orange

130 g orange marmalade

4 large eggs

150 g self-raising flour

75 g ground almonds

a 900-g loaf tin, greased and base-lined with baking parchment

SERVES 8–10

This is a moist cake streaked with zesty marmalade and kept a little squidgy by the addition of ground almonds. Be careful not to cook this in a very hot oven as the sugar content is high and the outside likes to brown. Serve it in chunky slices with Earl Grey tea.

Preheat the oven to 170°C (325°F) Gas 3.

Put the butter and sugar in a large mixing bowl and beat with an electric handheld whisk until the mixture is pale and light. Gradually add the orange juice, zest and the marmalade and swirl through with the whisk.

Lightly beat the eggs with a fork in a small bowl. Keep the electric whisk running in the creamed butter bowl and trickle the eggs in, 1 tablespoon at a time, beating thoroughly after each addition to stop them curdling. Finally, fold in the flour and ground almonds. Spoon the mixture into the prepared loaf tin and bake on a low shelf in the preheated oven for about 45 minutes, until lightly golden on top. A skewer inserted in the middle should come out clean.

Leave the loaf to cool in the tin for 15 minutes, then transfer to a wire rack to cool completely. It is easier to slice when it's cold – if you can resist its alluring aroma while it cools.

Crumpets

500 ml whole milk
1 teaspoon sugar
20 g fresh yeast or
  1 tablespoon dried
  active yeast
200 g strong white
  plain flour
200 g plain flour
1 teaspoon salt
2 tablespoons sunflower
  oil
250 ml hand-hot water
½ teaspoon bicarbonate
  of soda
4 x 8-cm metal rings,
  greased
MAKES 12

Making crumpets is like reverting back to the childhood days of chemistry sets – you may not understand the chemical reaction happening, but it's great to see the crumpets bubble, ready to receive melted butter in their pockets.

Pour the milk and sugar into a saucepan and heat until hand-hot. Remove from the heat, scatter over the yeast and set aside for 10 minutes until foamy on the surface.

Sift the flours and salt into a mixing bowl and add the wet, foamy mixture. Beat with an electric handheld whisk for a good 2–3 minutes, until smooth. Cover with clingfilm and leave in a draught-free place for 1½–2 hours, until it has doubled in size and is covered in tiny bubbles.

Mix the water and bicarbonate of soda until dissolved. Using the electric whisk, beat this into the risen dough until smooth. Cover again and leave to rise for a further 20 minutes.

Put the metal rings on a hot non-stick frying pan. Spoon 2 tablespoons of the batter into each ring so they are half full. Cook over very low heat for 5–7 minutes until the surface is pockmarked and dry around the edges. Slide the rings off, flip the crumpets over and cook for 1 minute, until pale gold. Wrap in a clean tea towel while you cook the rest. Serve with butter and a big pot of runny raspberry jam.

Poppyseed bagels

7 g dried active yeast
4 tablespoons clear honey
300 ml hand-hot water
450 g strong white plain
  flour
1 teaspoon salt
2 teaspoons bicarbonate
  of soda
2 tablespoons poppyseeds
a baking tray, lined with
  baking parchment
MAKES 10

Moist chewy bagels are made from a fairly standard white dough, but they are poached before being baked. I like to smother them in cream cheese and excessive amounts of raspberry jam for that sweet and savoury contrast.

Put the yeast in a small bowl with the honey and 100 ml of the water. Set aside for 10 minutes until frothy.

Put the flour and salt in a bowl and make a well in the centre. Pour in the frothy mixture and draw the flour into the liquid with a wooden spoon. Add more hand-hot water and continue to mix until you get a soft dough. It should not be very sticky. Turn out onto a lightly floured surface and knead for 10 minutes. Return to the bowl, cover and leave in a draught-free place for 20 minutes.

Divide the dough into 10 x 75-g pieces. Shape each piece into a flattish ball, then take a wooden spoon and use the handle to make a hole in the middle of each ball. Twirl the bagel around the spoon to make a hole 3 cm wide. It will close up on cooking, so exaggerate it. Lay the bagels on the baking tray and cover. Prove for 30–45 minutes.

Preheat the oven to 230°C (450°F) Gas 8. Bring a large pan of salted water to the boil and add the bicarbonate of soda. Poach 3 bagels at a time for 30 seconds on each side. Fish out, drain off any excess water and scatter with poppyseeds. Place on the baking tray. Bake for 10 minutes until lightly golden and cooked through.

Crumpets (right)

Sticky cinnamon & cardamom palmiers

6 cardamom pods

6 tablespoons demerara
    sugar

1 teaspoon ground
    cinnamon

4 tablespoons poppyseeds

375 g ready-made
    puff pastry

1 egg, beaten

a non-stick baking tray

MAKES 16

These little sugary pastries are ideal as a mid-morning snack with a strong black coffee. You can vary the spices or omit the cardamom and leave them plain.

Preheat the oven to 200°C (400°F) Gas 6.

Put the cardamom pods in a freezer bag and crush them to separate the pale green husks from the black seeds inside. Discard the husks and crush the seeds with the sugar using a pestle and mortar, just until they break up a little. Transfer to a small bowl with the ground cinnamon and poppyseeds.

Roll out the pastry on a lightly floured work surface into a rectangle approximately 60 × 30 cm. Brush all over with the beaten egg and scatter half the dry ingredients over the top. Fold the two shorter edges over to meet in the middle.

Brush with more egg wash and scatter with the remaining dry ingredients. Bring the new outside ends over again to join in the middle. Fold the pastry in half as if you were closing a book. Lift onto the non-stick baking tray, then gently press down so you have a rectangular log with pleated folds. Chill in the fridge for 30 minutes to firm up before slicing.

Remove from the fridge and cut into 1.5-cm slices. Return each slice, flat side down, to the baking tray with some room to expand. Bake in the preheated oven for 18–20 minutes, until golden. Leave to cool on a wire rack.

Jam & frangipane brioches

75 g unsalted butter, softened

75 g caster sugar

1 egg yolk

75 g ground almonds

75 g raspberry, rhubarb or apricot jam

6 stale brioche fingers or 4 stale brioche buns, halved

25 g flaked almonds

a baking tray, lined with baking parchment

MAKES 8–12

These are a cross between a Bakewell tart and an old French recipe for using up stale brioche, called Bostock. They are surprisingly easy to whip up and are wonderful for a decadent breakfast. They will keep for a couple of days and can be polished off at teatime or warmed and eaten with cream for a pudding.

Preheat the oven to 190°C (375°F) Gas 5.

To make what is effectively frangipane, put the butter and sugar in a bowl and beat with an electric handheld whisk until light and fluffy. Beat in the egg yolk in 2 stages (so that it doesn't curdle), then fold in the ground almonds.

Spread the jam over the cut sides of the brioche, then spread a blob of frangipane on top. Scatter with the flaked almonds. Transfer to the prepared baking tray and bake in the preheated oven for 10–12 minutes, until the topping is puffed up and tinged with brown.

Dairy-free banana, date & bran muffins

150 g wholemeal flour

100 g wheat bran

a pinch of salt

2 teaspoons ground
   cinnamon

2 teaspoons baking powder

2 eggs

75 g clear honey

200 ml soya milk

75 ml vegetable oil

150 g stoned dates,
   chopped

3 bananas, sliced

a 12-hole muffin tin

MAKES 10–12

These muffins are full of fibre and super filling. As with all muffins, they need to be stirred with a hand that is not too worried about getting every last lump out, as this rocky batter gives them their characteristically clumpy, rough texture.

Preheat the oven to 180°C (350°F) Gas 4. Line the muffin tin with paper cases.

Sift the flour, 80 g of the wheat bran, the salt, cinnamon and baking powder into a large mixing bowl.

Beat the eggs with the honey, soya milk and oil. Pour the wet ingredients into the dry ingredients and scatter the dates and bananas on top. Using a large spoon, fold until the mixture is moistened. It needs to be lumpy and shouldn't be overworked otherwise the baked muffins will be tough. Spoon into the paper cases until they are two-thirds full and scatter over the reserved bran. Bake in the preheated oven for 18–22 minutes.

Leave to cool in the tin for 5 minutes before transferring to a wire rack.

Exploding berry crumble muffins

375 g plain flour

3 teaspoons baking
   powder

1 teaspoon bicarbonate
   of soda

150 g golden caster sugar

½ teaspoon salt

2 eggs, beaten

115 g unsalted butter,
   melted

200 g soured cream

60 ml whole milk

180 g raspberries

TOPPING

100 g plain flour

75 g butter, chilled and
   cubed

30 g golden caster sugar

30 g flaked almonds

a 12-hole muffin tin

MAKES 12

These look like the muffins which are sold in cafés and which seem to have exploded out of their tins with their generous proportions. There is no secret trick to this – just fill the muffin cases up to the top.

Preheat the oven to 170°C (375°F) Gas 3. Line the muffin tin with paper cases and grease the surface of the tin where the muffins will rise and stick.

To make the topping, put the flour and butter in a food processor and pulse briefly, just until the butter is blended. Tip out into a bowl and add the sugar and almonds, pressing the mixture together with your hands.

To make the muffins, sift the flour, baking powder, bicarbonate of soda, sugar and salt into a large mixing bowl. Put the eggs in a small jug, add the melted butter, soured cream and milk and whisk to combine. Pour the wet ingredients into the dry ingredients and scatter the raspberries on top. Using a large spoon, fold until the mixture is moistened. It needs to be lumpy and shouldn't be overworked otherwise the baked muffins will be tough. Spoon into the paper cases right to the top. For regular-sized (not exploding!) muffins you can spoon the cases two-thirds full – you will be able to make more of these with this amount of mixture. Finish by scattering over the topping. Bake in the preheated oven for 25–28 minutes for large muffins, or 18–22 minutes for the smaller ones.

Leave to cool for 5 minutes in the tin before transferring to a wire rack.

Exploding berry crumble muffins (right)

Sugary jam doughnut muffins

75 g sunflower oil

150 g natural yoghurt

½ teaspoon vanilla extract

2 large eggs, beaten

275 g self-raising flour

½ teaspoon bicarbonate
of soda

a pinch of salt

100 g caster sugar

75 g blueberry jam

TOPPING

25 g unsalted butter,
melted

50 g caster sugar

*a 6-hole muffin tin,
lined with paper cases*

MAKES 6

This is a recipe for anyone who likes a warm sugary doughnut but dislikes the deep frying involved in making them. Of course the result is more cakey than bready but they are every bit as delicious, as they ooze jam and cover your lips with sugar crystals.

Preheat the oven to 190°C (375°F) Gas 5.

Put the oil, yoghurt, vanilla extract and eggs in a bowl and beat together.

In another, large bowl, mix together the flour, bicarbonate of soda, salt and sugar. Pour the wet ingredients into the dry ingredients and swiftly mix together, until just combined. It needs to be quite lumpy but you need to hassle any floury pockets until there are no more.

Drop 1 heaped tablespoon of the batter in each paper case. Make a dip in the mixture and spoon in a heaped teaspoon of the jam. Divide the remaining batter between the paper cases to cover the jam. Bake in the preheated oven for 18–20 minutes, until well risen. Set aside, still in the tin, to cool for 5 minutes before you apply the topping.

When the muffins have cooled for 5 minutes, brush their tops with the melted butter for the topping and roll in the sugar. Transfer to a wire rack to cool to room temperature.

Chocolate chip & peanut butter muffins

250 g plain flour

2 teaspoons baking powder

½ teaspoon bicarbonate
of soda

75 g caster sugar

250 g crunchy peanut
butter

1 large egg, beaten

50 g butter, melted

100 g natural yoghurt

100 ml whole milk

100 g milk chocolate chips

*a 12-hole muffin tin,
lined with paper cases*

MAKES 12

You can't really go wrong with salty peanuts and sweet chocolate. If you love Reese's Pieces, then this is the muffin you've been waiting for. For these indulgent muffins, I prefer the creamy sweetness of milk chocolate, rather than the more refined plain chocolate I usually use for baking.

Preheat the oven to 180°C (350°F) Gas 4.

Sift the flour, baking powder and bicarbonate of soda into a large mixing bowl, then add the sugar and crunchy peanut butter.

Put the egg, melted butter, yoghurt and milk in a bowl and beat together. Stir in the chocolate chips. Pour the wet ingredients into the dry ingredients. Using a large spoon, fold until the mixture is moistened. It needs to be lumpy and shouldn't be overworked otherwise the baked muffins will be tough. Spoon into the paper cases until they are two-thirds full. Bake in the preheated oven for 20–22 minutes, until golden and well risen.

Leave to cool in the tin for 5 minutes before transferring to a wire rack.

Sugary jam doughnut muffins (left)

Brioche french toast with pineapple & syrup

1 vanilla pod, split
lengthways

100 g light muscovado
sugar

2 cinnamon sticks

6 eggs, beaten

100 ml whole milk

8 slices of brioche loaf,
2 cm thick

25 g butter

3 tablespoons sunflower
oil

1 pineapple, peeled, cored
and sliced into rounds

SERVES 4

Light, buttery brioche makes wonderful French toast. As it is so rich, a slightly tart fruit is needed – I like to griddle slices of pineapple and drench them in syrup.

Scrape the seeds out of the vanilla pod. Put half the seeds, the pod, the sugar, 200 ml water and the cinnamon in a saucepan over low heat and heat gently until the sugar has dissolved. Turn up the heat and simmer for 10 minutes, until syrupy. Meanwhile, put the eggs, milk and remaining vanilla seeds in a wide bowl and whisk together lightly. Dip the brioche in the egg mixture, transfer to a plate and leave to soak up all the mixture.

Heat half the butter and oil in your largest frying pan over medium heat. Add as many slices of soaked bread as you can and cook for 2–3 minutes on each side. Repeat until all the bread is fried.

Heat a ridged griddle pan over high heat and brush the pineapple with a little of the syrup. Griddle for 2 minutes on each side. Serve 2 slices of French toast with a couple of slices of pineapple and a drizzle of the syrup.

Apple streusel coffee cake

150 g butter, softened

150 g golden caster sugar

2 large eggs, beaten

2 teaspoons vanilla extract

100 g plain flour, sifted

1/2 teaspoon baking powder

1/2 teaspoon bicarbonate
of soda

100 g ground almonds

100 g soured cream

3 dessert apples, peeled,
cored and sliced
1 cm thick

TOPPING

75 g plain flour

75 g light muscovado sugar

1/2 teaspoon ground
cinnamon

50 g butter, softened

100 g chopped pecan nuts

a 20-cm round cake tin

SERVES 8

This is a coffee cake in the sense that it is good with a mid-morning coffee. The cake mixture is really vanillary and stays a little bit moist around the apples as they let off their steam. I adore the contrast of this against the nutty, crunchy topping. A strong coffee and a gossip are all you need to accessorize this delight.

Preheat the oven to 180°C (350°F) Gas 4. Line the cake tin with baking parchment.

Cream the butter and sugar with an electric handheld whisk until fluffy. Gradually beat in the eggs and vanilla extract, then fold in the flour, baking powder, bicarbonate of soda and almonds. Beat in the soured cream until you have a dropping consistency. Spoon half the batter into the prepared tin. Arrange the apples snugly on top, in a single layer, and spoon over the remaining batter.

To make the topping, put the flour, sugar and cinnamon in a bowl and rub in the butter with your fingertips until the mixture is crumbly. Add 1 tablespoon water and the pecan nuts and break into lumps with a blunt knife. Scatter this over the cake and bake in the preheated oven for 50–60 minutes. A skewer inserted in the middle of the cake should come out clean. If it doesn't, bake for a few minutes more before checking again (noting that the apples will make it seem quite wet).

Leave the cake to cool in the tin for 10 minutes, then transfer to a wire rack to cool completely. Alternatively, enjoy it with cream while it is still warm.

Apple streusel coffee cake (right)

Pecan & maple syrup sticky buns

250 ml whole milk,
plus extra for glazing
85 g unsalted butter
500 g strong white
plain flour
50 g light muscovado sugar
7 g easy-blend dried yeast
½ teaspoon salt
1 egg, beaten

FILLING
75 g unsalted butter,
softened
75 ml maple syrup
75 g light muscovado sugar
1 tablespoon ground
cinnamon
100 g chopped pecan nuts
MAKES ABOUT 16

It's quite fun to make your own sticky buns, but you need to start the day before unless you are a hopeless insomniac. This dough is enriched with butter and egg and is ready to bake when it is like a soft, puffy marshmallow. Try putting different nuts, chocolate chips and/or dried fruit in the centre for a change. They are best served warm on the day they are made, so if you are eating them after that, warm them a little in the oven first to soften up.

Put the milk and butter in a saucepan and heat gently until the butter has melted. Remove from the heat and leave to cool until blood temperature. Put the flour, sugar, yeast and salt in a large bowl.

Pour the egg into the cooled milk and beat. Make a well in the centre of the dry ingredients and pour in the milk mixture. Gradually draw in the floury mixture with a wooden spoon until it is all combined. Bring the dough together with your hands, then tip out onto a lightly floured work surface and knead for 10 minutes, until smooth and the dough springs back when poked. Place in a lightly oiled bowl and cover with clingfilm. Leave to rise for 1–2 hours.

Meanwhile, to make the filling, mix the butter, maple syrup, sugar and cinnamon in a small bowl and set aside.

Push the air out of the dough and lay it on the work surface. Using the heel of your hand, flatten and shape it into a rectangle about 30 x 40 cm. Spread the filling over the surface of the dough. With one of the long sides facing you, roll up the dough like a Swiss roll and chill in the fridge for 1 hour.

Cut the roll into 2-cm slices. Arrange these, flat side down, on a baking tray spaced about 2 cm apart so that they have room to expand. Cover loosely with clingfilm and leave to rise for 30 minutes, until puffy. Meanwhile, preheat the oven to 200°C (400°F) Gas 6.

Brush the buns with milk and slide into the oven. Immediately reduce the heat to 180°C (350°F) Gas 4 and bake for 12–15 minutes, until cooked through and golden.

Churros with cinnamon sugar

50 g butter

2 tablespoons golden
   caster sugar

125 g plain flour

a pinch of salt

2 large eggs, beaten

about 750 ml vegetable oil,
   for deep frying

CINNAMON SUGAR

6 tablespoons golden
   caster sugar

1 teaspoon ground
   cinnamon

*a piping bag, fitted with a
   1.5-cm star-shaped nozzle*

MAKES 12

These Spanish morsels of deliciousness are a bit like doughnuts. Making them is a little like making French choux pastry, except that the batter is then squeezed out of a piping bag into boiling hot oil. I know this all sounds like a labour of love but there is nothing better on a rainy day than to enjoy them with a cup of hot chocolate. When they cool down, they lose a lot of their magic.

Put the butter, sugar and 150 ml water in a small saucepan and bring to the boil. Tip the flour and salt into the boiling water, remove from the heat and beat vigorously with a wooden spoon for 20 seconds, until the mixture comes away from the sides of the pan and forms a clump. Leave to cool for 10 minutes or until it is lukewarm. Beat in the eggs, a spoonful at a time, as you would a sponge cake. Cover, chill in the fridge and leave to cool completely.

Fill a large saucepan one-third full with vegetable oil. Heat to 190°C (or until a

dot of the churros batter bubbles up and floats straightaway). Spoon the batter into the prepared piping bag. Squeeze 3 × 9-cm lengths of batter into the hot oil. (Use your finger to release the batter from the nozzle of the piping bag.) Fry for 2 minutes on each side until golden. Drain on kitchen paper and fry the remaining batter in the same way.

To make the cinnamon sugar, mix the sugar and cinnamon in a large, wide dish. Roll the churros in the mixture while they are hot and oily, until evenly coated. Serve with hot chocolate or coffee.

Apple turnovers

25 g unsalted butter

100 g demerara sugar

2 Bramley apples, peeled,
   cored and roughly
   chopped

¼ teaspoon ground nutmeg

½ teaspoon ground
   cinnamon

finely grated zest of
   1 unwaxed lemon

1 tablespoon freshly
   squeezed lemon juice

375 g ready-made
   puff pastry

1 egg yolk mixed with
   1 tablespoon milk

*a baking tray, lightly dusted
   with flour*

MAKES 6

These are quick to whip up. You can even use a shop-bought spiced apple purée for a cheat's version. If you are lucky enough to know someone who has a Bramley apple tree, you would be doing them a favour to make use of their windfall, so reserve this recipe for the autumn, for times such as these.

Preheat the oven to 200°C (400°F) Gas 6.

Put the butter and 75 g of the sugar in a saucepan over medium heat and leave until the butter has melted. Add the apples, nutmeg, cinnamon and lemon zest and juice. Cover with a lid and stir occasionally for 3–4 minutes, until the apple wedges gracefully collapse into a chunky purée. Set aside to cool slightly.

Roll out the pastry on a lightly floured work surface until it is ½ cm thick. Trim any curvy edges into straight lines, then cut into about 6 × 10-cm squares.

Spoon a dollop of the apple purée in the centre of each pastry square.

Brush the edges with egg wash. Fold over one corner so it meets with the other and press gently. Crimp the edges with a fork or your fingers to seal in the filling. Using a sharp knife, slit the top 4 or 5 times to allow the steam to escape and stop the pastry going soggy. Transfer the turnovers to the prepared baking tray and glaze with egg wash. Sprinkle the remaining sugar over the top. Bake in the preheated oven for 20 minutes, until golden and puffed up.

Leave to cool for just a few moments before devouring (without burning your mouth on the hot filling!), or eat cold.

pancakes & waffles

Potato & rosemary pancakes with bacon & honey Buckwheat crêpes with mushrooms, caramelized onions, bacon & gruyère **Blinis with smoked salmon & crème fraîche** Sweet potato pancakes with hot smoked trout & chilli-lime butter Orange cornmeal hotcakes with orange flower syrup **Blueberry pancakes** Apricot pancakes with maple & pecan butter Lemon ricotta pancakes with blackberries **Buckwheat & banana pancakes** Dairy-free coconut pancakes with lime syrup & mango Buttermilk waffles with crème fraîche, bitter chocolate sauce & hazelnuts **Gingerbread waffles with strawberries**

Potato & rosemary pancakes with bacon & honey

500 g potatoes, peeled
1 tablespoon finely chopped
fresh rosemary needles
150 g plain flour
½ teaspoon bicarbonate
of soda
275 ml buttermilk
12 rashers of streaky
bacon
25 g butter
sea salt and freshly ground
black pepper
clear honey, to serve
SERVES 4

These pancakes are based on the Irish potato dish called boxty, in which some of the potatoes are cooked and mashed, and the others are grated to give the pancakes a bit of texture on top of the fluffiness. They were obviously once seen as a sign of domesticity, as they prompted the saying: 'Boxty on the griddle, boxty in the pan, if you can't make boxty, you'll never get a man'.

Put 300 g of the potatoes in a saucepan of cold, salted water and bring to the boil. Cook for 20–25 minutes, until soft. Drain and mash, then season and add the rosemary. Leave to cool.

Meanwhile, peel and grate the remaining potatoes and leave them raw. Put both sets of potato in a mixing bowl and beat in the flour and bicarbonate of soda, then the buttermilk.

Preheat the grill.

Grill the bacon until well done (there's no need to turn it over while it's being grilled). Leave to cool for 4–5 minutes, until crisp. Turn off the grill and keep the bacon in a low oven while you continue cooking.

Heat half the butter in a frying pan over low/medium heat and wait for it to sizzle. Drop 2–3 ladlefuls of the batter into the pan, spaced apart, and spread out with a spatula. They need about 3 minutes on the first side, then a little less on the other side. Keep warm with the bacon in the oven while you cook the rest.

Serve 2–3 pancakes per person, with a few rashers of bacon and some honey to drizzle over.

Buckwheat crêpes with mushrooms, caramelized onions, bacon & gruyère

50 g buckwheat flour

50 g plain flour

1 large egg

150 ml whole milk

sunflower oil, for frying

sea salt and freshly ground
    black pepper

FILLING

25 g butter

2 large red onions, sliced

sprig of fresh thyme

200 g chestnut
    mushrooms, sliced

200 g smoked bacon
    lardons

2 garlic cloves, sliced

100 g Gruyère cheese,
    grated

150 ml crème fraîche

a 22-cm frying pan

SERVES 4

This is a classic combination from Normandy. Make sure your batter is thin enough to run over the pan easily or you'll end up with crêpes that are not delicate and lacy, but thick and stodgy.

Mix the flours and a large pinch of salt in a mixing bowl and make a well in the centre. Beat the egg and milk in a small bowl, and pour into the flours. Gradually draw the flour into the liquid with a wooden spoon until smooth. Cover and chill in the fridge for 1 hour.

Preheat the oven to low.

Whisk 80 ml cold water into the rested batter – it should now be the consistency of single cream.

To make the filling, heat the butter in a frying pan over low heat. Stir in the onions and thyme, season with black pepper, cover and cook for 10 minutes, until the onion has softened. Turn up the heat and add the mushrooms, bacon and garlic. Stir for 6–8 minutes, until lightly caramelized. Stir in the Gruyère and crème fraîche and remove from the heat.

Heat your 22-cm frying pan over medium heat. Grease the pan with a piece of kitchen paper dipped in oil. Pour in 3 tablespoons of the batter, swirl to coat the base of the pan and cook for 1 minute on each side. Keep warm in the oven while you cook the rest.

Reheat the filling until bubbling and smooth (remove the thyme sprig), season, then divide between the crêpes.

Blinis with smoked salmon & crème fraîche

50 g buckwheat flour

50 g strong plain
    white flour

1 teaspoon salt

125 ml whole milk

75 ml crème fraîche,
    plus extra to serve

5 g fresh yeast, crumbled,
    or 7 g dried active yeast

1 large egg, separated

sunflower oil, for frying

smoked salmon, to serve

snipped chives (optional)

MAKES 20 SMALL BLINIS

It's worth making your own fresh blinis because their flavour is much more complex than the ready-made kind. You can make the batter the night before, then let it have its final rising half an hour before cooking. They freeze well too.

Sift the flours and salt into a large mixing bowl. Heat the milk in a saucepan until hand hot. Add the crème fraîche and yeast and stir until smooth. Pour onto the flours with the egg yolk and stir well to blend. Cover and leave to rise for 1 hour.

Beat the egg white with an electric handheld whisk until soft peaks form. Fold into the batter, cover and leave for 30 minutes. Preheat the oven to low.

To make the blinis, heat a heavy-based frying pan over medium heat. Grease with a piece of kitchen paper dipped in oil. Drop in 2 tablespoons of the batter. After 30 seconds bubbles will appear on the surface. Flip the blini over and cook for 30 seconds on the other side. Keep warm in the oven while you cook the rest. Serve with crème fraîche, smoked salmon, chives, if using, and black pepper.

Blinis with smoked salmon & crème fraîche (left)

Sweet potato pancakes with hot smoked trout & chilli-lime butter

250 g sweet potato, peeled

3 tablespoons sunflower oil, plus extra for frying

225 ml whole milk

1 egg

130 g plain flour

2 teaspoons baking powder

a pinch of cayenne pepper

2 teaspoons fish sauce

225 g hot smoked trout

fresh coriander, to garnish

CHILLI-LIME BUTTER

2 spring onions, sliced

1 red chilli, shredded

1 teaspoon grated fresh ginger

1 teaspoon demerara sugar

2 teaspoons fish sauce

freshly squeezed juice of 2 limes

75 g butter

SERVES 4

This makes a delicious Thai-inspired brunch dish. The sweet potato helps to keep the pancakes beautifully moist and using fish sauce instead of salt adds another Thai-style touch. The chilli-lime butter soaks into the pancakes and really brings out the flavour of the sweet potato. Even if the dish sounds a little novel to you, try it because all the flavours work beautifully and it makes a change from the usual maple syrup and pancake combination.

Preheat the oven to low.

Halve the sweet potato and put in a saucepan of boiling water. Simmer for 25 minutes until really soft. Test with a knife to check it is evenly cooked.

Drain the potatoes and mash with the oil. Stir in the milk and leave the mixture to cool before beating in the egg. Sift in the flour, baking powder and cayenne pepper, and season with the fish sauce instead of salt. Set aside.

To make the chilli-lime butter, mix the spring onions, chilli, ginger, sugar, fish sauce and lime juice and set aside.

Heat a frying pan or flat griddle pan over medium heat. Grease the pan with a piece of kitchen paper dipped in oil. Drop in 2 tablespoons of the potato batter and cook for 2 minutes on the first side, until bubbles appear and the edges are dry. Flip over and cook on the other side for a further 2 minutes. Keep warm in the oven while you cook the rest.

Melt the butter for the chilli-lime butter in a saucepan and stir in the reserved dressing. Serve the pancakes topped with trout and coriander, and pour over the warm chilli-lime butter.

Orange cornmeal hotcakes with orange flower syrup

150 ml buttermilk

2 eggs, separated

50 ml freshly squeezed orange juice

finely grated zest of ½ orange

50 g cornmeal or polenta

50 g plain flour

3 tablespoons soft brown sugar

1 teaspoon baking powder

a pinch of salt

melted butter, to serve

ORANGE FLOWER SYRUP

120 ml maple syrup

a drop of orange flower water

SERVES 4

These pancakes have a citrusy tang to them and a slightly granular crunch from the cornmeal. The maple syrup is spiked with a small drop of fragrant orange flower water, but a little bit of butter on the hotcakes first won't go amiss.

Preheat the oven to low.

To make the orange flower syrup, stir the maple syrup and orange flower water together in a small bowl.

Put the buttermilk, egg yolks, orange juice and zest in a mixing bowl and beat together. Add the cornmeal, flour, sugar, baking powder and salt and fold in until just moistened. Do not overmix otherwise you will toughen the texture.

Whisk the egg whites in a separate bowl with an electric handheld whisk until soft peaks form. Using a large metal spoon, fold the whites into the batter.

Wipe a frying pan with a piece of kitchen paper dipped in melted butter. Heat up, then drop in 2–3 tablespoons of the batter. Cook for 2 minutes, until bubbles appear on the top and the edges are dry. Cook in batches of 3 or whatever fits comfortably in your pan. Flip the hotcake over and cook for 2 minutes on the other side.

Serve about 3 hotcakes per person. Put some melted butter on each hotcake and serve with the orange flower syrup.

Blueberry pancakes

125 g self-raising flour

1 teaspoon baking powder

2 tablespoons caster sugar

¼ teaspoon salt

1 egg

100 ml whole milk

50 g butter, melted

150 g blueberries, plus extra to serve

maple syrup, to serve

SERVES 4

Perfect blueberry pancakes should be light and fluffy, with a good rise on them. The secret is to use some water – an all-milk batter makes the pancakes heavier. And remember to serve them with lashings of maple syrup.

Preheat the oven to low.

Sift the flour and baking powder into a large mixing bowl and stir in the sugar and salt. Put the egg, milk and 75 ml water in a jug and beat to combine.

Stir half the butter into the wet ingredients in the jug. Mix the wet ingredients with the dry ingredients until no lumps of flour remain.

Wipe a heavy-based frying pan with a scrunched-up piece of kitchen paper dipped in the remaining melted butter. Heat up, then drop in 4 tablespoons of the batter. Cook for 1–2 minutes on the first side, then scatter over a few of the blueberries and flip the pancake over. Cook for 2 minutes, until golden and cooked through. Keep warm in the oven while you make the rest.

Serve with more blueberries and lashings of maple syrup.

Blueberry pancakes (left)

Apricot pancakes with maple & pecan butter

125 g self-raising flour

1 teaspoon baking powder

2 tablespoons caster sugar

50 g butter, melted

¼ teaspoon salt

1 egg

150 ml whole milk

4 apricots, stoned and
 roughly chopped

MAPLE & PECAN BUTTER

25 g shelled pecan nuts,
 chopped

75 g butter, softened

2 tablespoons maple syrup

SERVES 4

Soft stone fruit works beautifully with fluffy pancakes, but make sure they are really soft and ripe. Apricots are among my favourite fruit, with their sweet perfumed flesh and inoffensively furry skin.

Preheat the oven to low.

To make the maple & pecan butter, put the pecans in a dry frying pan over medium heat and leave them to heat up. Stir so they brown evenly, then remove from the heat.

Beat the butter and maple syrup together. It may take a while to come together but once it warms up enough it will blend smoothly. Stir in the toasted pecans and set aside.

Sift the flour and baking powder in a large mixing bowl and stir in the sugar and salt. Put half the butter, the egg, milk and 75 ml water in a jug and beat to combine. Mix the wet ingredients with the dry ingredients until no lumps of flour remain.

Wipe a heavy-based frying pan with a scrunched-up piece of kitchen paper dipped in melted butter. Heat up, then drop in 2–3 tablespoons of batter on one side of the pan and the same on the other side of the pan. Cook for about 1–2 minutes on the first side, until the edges look dry, then scatter over some apricots and flip over. Cook for 2 minutes, until golden and cooked through. Keep warm in the oven while you make the rest. Serve with the maple & pecan butter.

Lemon ricotta pancakes with blackberries

250 g ricotta

freshly squeezed juice
 and grated zest of
 1 unwaxed lemon

3 eggs, separated

50 g butter, melted

100 g plain flour

1 teaspoon bicarbonate
 of soda

a pinch of salt

4 tablespoons caster sugar

blackberries and crème
 fraîche, to serve

SERVES 4

These pancakes are very fluffy and light. They need cooking slowly as they are so delicate. You can turn them into savoury pancakes by omitting the sugar and folding through some chopped green herbs, such as chives and tarragon, then serving with smoked salmon instead of blackberries.

Preheat the oven to low.

Put the ricotta, lemon juice and zest, egg yolks and half the butter in a mixing bowl and beat together. Sift in the flour, bicarbonate of soda and salt and fold in. Whisk the egg whites in a separate bowl with an electric handheld whisk until soft peaks form. Add the sugar and whisk until glossy and firm. Using a large metal spoon, fold the whites into the batter.

Wipe a heavy-based frying pan with a scrunched-up piece of kitchen paper dipped in the melted butter. Drop a heaped tablespoon of batter in the pan to make a 6-cm circle. Cook in batches of 3 or 4 depending on the size of the pan. Cook for 2 minutes on each side until risen and cooked through. Keep warm in the oven while you make the rest. Serve with blackberries and crème fraîche.

Lemon ricotta pancakes with blackberries (right)

Buckwheat & banana pancakes

75 g buckwheat flour

40 g plain flour

1 teaspoon bicarbonate of soda

¼ teaspoon salt

2 tablespoons clear honey, plus extra to serve

2 eggs, separated

250 ml soured cream

sunflower oil, for frying

2 bananas, sliced

SERVES 4

The bananas in these pancakes become caramelized in the hot pan, and when you drizzle over some honey before serving, everything becomes even sweeter.

Preheat the oven to low.

Sift the flours, bicarbonate of soda and salt into a large mixing bowl. Put the honey, egg yolks and soured cream in a jug and beat to combine. Mix the wet ingredients with the dry ingredients until no lumps of flour remain. Whisk the egg whites in a separate bowl with an electric handheld whisk until soft peaks form. Using a large metal spoon, fold the whites into the batter.

Heat a heavy-based frying pan over medium heat. Grease the pan with a piece of kitchen paper dipped in oil. Drop 2–3 tablespoons of batter into the pan. Cook for 1–2 minutes on the first side, until the edges look dry, then scatter over 3–4 slices of banana and flip the pancake over. Cook for 2 minutes, until golden and cooked through. Keep warm in the oven while you make the rest. Serve with honey, for drizzling.

Dairy-free coconut pancakes with lime syrup & mango

150 g plain flour

3 teaspoons baking powder

¼ teaspoon salt

2 tablespoons demerara sugar

3 tablespoons desiccated coconut

200 ml coconut milk

2 tablespoons sunflower oil, plus extra for frying

1 mango, peeled, stoned and sliced

LIME SYRUP

freshly squeezed juice of 3 limes

grated zest of 1 lime

100 g clear honey

6 cardamom pods, crushed

SERVES 4

These pancakes are completely dairy free; they don't even contain egg. This makes them a bit more dense but as they are drenched in a runny lime and honey syrup before serving, this is soon taken care of. Try to find the ripest, most perfumed mango to make this dish exquisite.

Preheat the oven to low.

To make the lime syrup, put the lime juice and zest, honey and cardamom pods in a small saucepan and bring to the boil. Boil for 5 minutes, then remove from the heat and set aside.

Meanwhile, sift the flour, baking powder and salt into a large mixing bowl and stir in the sugar and desiccated coconut. Put the coconut milk, 75 ml water and the oil in a jug and beat to combine. Mix the wet ingredients with the dry ingredients until no lumps of flour remain.

Heat a heavy-based frying pan over medium heat. Grease the pan with a piece of kitchen paper dipped in oil. Drop 2–3 tablespoons of batter into the pan. Cook for 1–2 minutes on each side until golden and cooked through. Keep warm in the oven while you make the rest. Serve with mango and lime syrup.

Dairy-free coconut pancakes with lime syrup & mango (left)

Buttermilk waffles with crème fraîche, bitter chocolate sauce & hazelnuts

150 g plain flour

½ teaspoon bicarbonate of soda

1 teaspoon baking powder

3 tablespoons caster sugar

2 eggs

1 teaspoon vanilla extract

50 g unsalted butter, melted, plus extra for cooking

275 ml buttermilk

25 g chopped hazelnuts

crème fraîche, to serve

BITTER CHOCOLATE SAUCE

100 g plain chocolate

15 g butter

a waffle iron

SERVES 4

It is fairly indulgent to go for waffles with chocolate and crème fraîche before you have even ventured out into the world, but now and again, it's good to be decadent! The sauce is so easy and making it with water rather than cream is not a thrifty cheat, but a way of bringing out the bitterness in the chocolate.

Preheat the oven to low.

Sift the flour, bicarbonate of soda and baking powder into a large mixing bowl. Put the sugar, eggs, vanilla extract, butter, buttermilk and 50 ml water in a jug and beat to combine. Pour the wet ingredients into the dry ingredients and whisk until blended. Don't worry about any small lumps. Set aside.

To make the bitter chocolate sauce, put the chocolate, butter and 80 ml water in a heatproof bowl over a saucepan of gently simmering water. Do not let the base of the bowl touch the water. Leave to melt for 5 minutes. Remove from the heat and stir until smooth. Keep warm on the pan. Meanwhile, put the hazelnuts in a dry frying pan over medium heat and leave them to heat up. Stir so they brown evenly, then remove from the heat.

When you're ready to cook the waffles, heat your waffle iron and grease with oil. Ladle in enough batter to fill it, then close. Check the manufacturer's instructions for cooking times, but it should need about 3–5 minutes. When ready, steam will stop escaping from the sides and the waffles will look crisp and golden. Keep warm in the oven while you cook the rest. Serve hot with crème fraîche, a drizzle of chocolate sauce and a scattering of toasted hazelnuts.

Gingerbread waffles with strawberries

150 g plain flour

½ teaspoon bicarbonate
   of soda

1 teaspoon baking powder

1 teaspoon ground
   cinnamon

1 teaspoon ground ginger

⅛ teaspoon ground nutmeg

50 g molasses

2 eggs

50 g unsalted butter,
   melted, plus extra
   for cooking

200 ml whole milk

clear honey and
   strawberries, to serve

a waffle iron

MAKES 8–12

Depending on the size and shape of your waffle iron, this recipe will make a batch of 8 or much more if your waffle maker makes thin ones. If you don't have such a contraption (not everyone feels the need for a waffle maker in their lives), you can make these into pancakes by simply cooking them in a heavy-based frying pan or on a flat griddle.

Preheat the oven to low.

Sift the flour, bicarbonate of soda, baking powder and spices in a large mixing bowl. Put the molasses, eggs, butter and milk in a jug and beat to combine. Pour the wet ingredients into the dry ingredients and beat to combine. Don't worry about any small lumps.

Heat your waffle iron and grease with oil. Ladle in enough batter to fill it, then close. Check the manufacturer's instructions for cooking times, but it should need about 3–5 minutes. When ready, steam will stop escaping from the sides and the waffles will look crisp and golden. Keep warm in the oven while you cook the rest. Serve hot with honey and a handful of the sweetest strawberries.

mains

Baked tomatoes stuffed with goats' cheese & herbs Pancetta, taleggio, roasted leek & onion tart **Cheesy polenta with sausages & red onions** English breakfast quiche Courgette fritters with tomato & feta salad **Garlic mushrooms & goats' cheese on sourdough toast** Corn cakes with bacon & avocado Crab cakes with slaw & sweet chilli sauce **Hot smoked salmon hash with dill crème fraîche** Sweet potato, chorizo & fried egg hash Dukkah & harissa sausage rolls **Smoked haddock kedgeree** Linguine with lemon, basil & parmesan cream

Baked tomatoes stuffed with goats' cheese & herbs

4 large, stuffing tomatoes
such as Marmande or
heirloom, or more of
a smaller variety

2 tablespoons extra virgin
olive oil, plus extra
to drizzle

1 onion, finely chopped

1 tablespoon chopped
fresh thyme leaves

200 g goats' cheese

4 tablespoons dried
breadcrumbs

2 eggs, beaten

a handful of fresh basil
leaves

SERVES 4

Stuffed tomatoes are quite an old-fashioned idea, but I was reminded just how delectable they can be on a recent trip to France. When you see the quirky-looking shapes of the Marmande and heirloom tomatoes in their various shades of green and orange, that's the time to make this dish. The secret is to slightly undercook them so the tomatoes don't just collapse into amoeba-like blobs. I like to use quite a strong aged goats' cheese for this, as it contrasts against the sweetness of the tomatoes when they are cooked.

Preheat the oven to 180°C (350°F) Gas 4.

Slice the top third off the tomatoes and reserve. Using a melon baller, scoop out the seeds and juices and discard or reserve for making a tomato sauce.

Heat the oil in a frying pan, add the onion and thyme and soften for 5 minutes. Leave to cool slightly.

In a mixing bowl, beat the goats' cheese, breadcrumbs and eggs together and season well. Stir in the onion mixture and a few of the basil leaves. Divide the stuffing between the hollow tomatoes and top with the reserved tomato hats. Arrange in a baking dish, drizzle with oil and scatter over the remaining basil leaves. Bake in the preheated oven for 18–20 minutes.

Pancetta, taleggio, roasted leek & onion tart

2 leeks, sliced 2 cm thick

2 red onions, peeled and
cut into slim wedges

2 tablespoons extra virgin
olive oil, plus extra
to drizzle

1 tablespoon balsamic
vinegar

375 g ready-rolled
puff pastry

150 g Taleggio (rind
removed), cubed

8 wafer-thin slices
of pancetta

50 g rocket

sea salt and freshly ground
black pepper

SERVES 4–6

Roasted leeks are one of my favourite ways with vegetables. I love that they are sweet and crispy at the same time. They go brilliantly atop a tart, needing only creamy cheese to finish them off. I have used the soft, slightly stinky Taleggio in this version, but you could just as easily use a blue cheese or mozzarella.

Preheat the oven to 200°C (400°F) Gas 6.

Put the leeks, onions, oil and balsamic vinegar in a roasting tray and season. Toss well, then roast in the preheated oven for 30–35 minutes, until soft. Leave the oven on for the tart.

Meanwhile, unroll the ready-rolled puff pastry, lay it on a baking tray and prick all over with a fork.

When the roasting vegetables are soft and slightly charred, scatter them evenly over the pastry. Drop the cubed Taleggio all over, then drape the pancetta slices over everything. Bake in the oven for 25–30 minutes until the pastry is golden and well risen at the edges. Strew the rocket over the top and drizzle with a little extra olive oil before serving.

Cheesy polenta with sausages & red onions

12 pork sausages

2 red onions, peeled and
cut into slim wedges

a handful of fresh
sage leaves

6 tablespoons olive oil

150 g instant polenta

1 tablespoon chopped
fresh thyme leaves

50 g Parmesan, grated

200 g feta, crumbled

sea salt and freshly ground
black pepper

a 20-cm square tin, greased

SERVES 4

If you are not yet sold on polenta, I urge you to try this method of preparation because it has converted many a person. The secret is that it needs to be seasoned well and enriched with lots of cheese, as well as being fried over high heat until golden so that you get the crunchy exterior and the soft creaminess inside.

Preheat the oven to 190°C (375°F) Gas 5.

Put the sausages and onions in a roasting tray. Scatter the sage over the top and drizzle with 2 tablespoons of the oil, then toss everything together. Roast in the preheated oven for 30–35 minutes, until golden and cooked through.

Bring 650 ml water to the boil with a pinch of salt and 1 tablespoon of the oil. Remove from the heat and pour in the polenta. Mix it with a wooden spoon and lots of elbow grease. Return to low heat

for about 2–3 minutes, stirring constantly. Remove from the heat, beat in the thyme and cheeses and season generously. Spoon into the prepared tin and smooth out the surface. Leave to cool and set.

Tip the polenta onto a board and quarter, then cut each quarter in half to make triangles. Heat a frying pan over high heat and add the remaining oil. Add as many polenta triangles as you can and fry for 2–3 minutes on each side, until golden. Serve with the sausage mixture.

Cheesy polenta with sausages & red onions (left)

English breakfast quiche

Here are all the flavours of a traditional full farmhouse English fry-up in a quiche. Bake it the day before a long, early-morning journey when you have to have your breakfast on the go. Try to resist smothering it in ketchup!

PASTRY

225 g plain flour

1 teaspoon English
   mustard powder

150 g butter, chilled
   and cubed

1 egg, beaten

FILLING

4 pork sausages

200 g cherry tomatoes,
   halved

200 g bacon lardons

200 g button mushrooms,
   halved

1 tablespoon olive oil

300 ml crème fraîche

3 large eggs, beaten

1 teaspoon English
   mustard powder

*a 25-cm fluted, loose-
   bottomed tart tin*

baking beans

SERVES 6

Preheat the oven to 200°C (400°F) Gas 6.

To make the pastry, put the flour, mustard powder and butter in a food processor and pulse until they are just combined. Add the egg and run the motor until the mixture just comes into a ball. Turn out, wrap with clingfilm and chill in the fridge for 30 minutes.

To make the filling, put the sausages in a roasting tray and roast in the preheated oven for 10 minutes. Take the tray out of the oven, throw in the tomatoes, bacon and mushrooms, drizzle over the oil and return to the oven to roast for 15–20 minutes, until everything is tender and cooked through. Leave the oven on.

Roll out the pastry on a lightly floured surface until it is about 3 mm thick and use to line the tart tin. Press the pastry into the corners and leave the overhang. Prick the base all over with a fork, line with baking parchment and fill with baking beans. Bake in the oven for 8 minutes, then remove the beans and paper. Trim off the overhang and reduce the heat to 150°C (300°F) Gas 2. Return the pastry case to the oven for 2–3 minutes to dry out while you prepare the filling.

To finish the filling, slice the sausages and scatter them with the rest of the roasted ingredients into the pastry case. Mix the crème fraîche, eggs and mustard powder and pour over everything in the pastry case. Bake for 30–35 minutes, until set around the edges. Turn off the oven and leave the tart to cool in the oven, with the door open, for 15 minutes. Cut into slices and serve warm or cold.

Courgette fritters with tomato & feta salad

3 courgettes, grated
½ red onion, finely chopped
1 teaspoon cumin seeds
2 red chillies, finely chopped
75 g plain flour
½ teaspoon bicarbonate
 of soda
2 tablespoons fresh mint
 leaves, chopped
2 eggs, beaten
4 tablespoons olive oil

TOMATO & FETA SALAD
1 tablespoon red wine
 vinegar
½ teaspoon English
 mustard powder
3 tablespoons olive oil
3 tomatoes, chopped
4 spring onions, sliced
200 g feta, crumbled
SERVES 4

These little fritters are a great way of using up courgettes if you have a glut of them in your garden. The courgettes are salted in order to remove some of the moisture (not the bitterness), otherwise they can be quite soggy. Deseed the chillies for the fritters if you don't like the heat. You can serve the fritters with this tomato & feta salad or just a simple yoghurt and mint dip, if you prefer.

Preheat the oven to low.

Put the courgettes and a good pinch of salt in a colander. Toss well to distribute the salt and leave for 20 minutes. Squeeze the courgettes to extract some of the moisture, then pat dry with kitchen paper.

Mix the courgettes with the onion, cumin seeds, chillies, flour, bicarbonate of soda, mint and eggs in a mixing bowl. The mixture will seem quite dry at first but the courgettes will moisten everything the more you stir. Season and leave for 10 minutes while you make the tomato & feta salad.

To make the tomato & feta salad, whisk together the vinegar and mustard powder, then add the oil and whisk until it emulsifies. Season. Put the tomatoes, spring onions, feta and dressing in a dish.

Heat the oil in a non-stick frying pan over medium/high heat. Drop a heaped tablespoon of batter into the pan. Cook in batches of 3–4 depending on the size of the pan. Cook for 2–3 minutes on each side, until really golden and cooked through. Keep warm in the oven while you cook the rest. Serve with a mound of the tomato & feta salad.

Garlic mushrooms & goats' cheese on sourdough toast

8 field mushrooms
3 garlic cloves, crushed
3 tablespoons olive oil
25 g pine nuts
2 tablespoons balsamic
 vinegar
4 slices of sourdough
 bread
150 g fresh goats' cheese
fresh tarragon, to serve
sea salt and freshly ground
 black pepper
SERVES 4

Garlicky mushrooms are great for breakfast, but try them on a layer of soft, creamy goats' cheese and you will be in utter heaven. The kind of cheese you are looking for is a soft fresh cheese, not aged, so it will not have a rind. You could also use ricotta if you like. Seek out a good, sturdy rustic bread such as sourdough for this dish to prevent the underneath going soggy.

Preheat the oven to 200°C (400°F) Gas 6.

Put the mushrooms, garlic and oil in a roasting tray. Toss well and season. Roast in the preheated oven for 15 minutes, until tender. Stir in the pine nuts and balsamic vinegar halfway through roasting.

Just before the mushrooms are ready, toast the slices of sourdough bread and spread with the goats' cheese. Place the mushrooms on top, stalk side up, scatter with the tarragon and serve immediately. Add more seasoning, if necessary.

Garlic mushrooms & goats' cheese on sourdough toast (left)

Corn cakes with bacon & avocado

75 g self-raising flour
30 g cornmeal or polenta
½ teaspoon bicarbonate
    of soda
a pinch of cayenne pepper
2 large eggs
150 ml soured cream
400 g tinned sweetcorn
    (drained weight)
3 spring onions, sliced
12 rashers of bacon
sunflower oil, for frying
1 avocado, stoned and sliced
a small handful of rocket
sea salt and freshly ground
    black pepper
SERVES 4

If you are veering towards lunch rather than breakfast, you could serve this with a mound of baby spinach and rocket dressed in lemon and olive oil and perhaps a few roasted peppers strewn amongst the greens to make it more substantial.

Preheat the grill.

Put the flour, cornmeal, bicarbonate of soda and cayenne pepper in a mixing bowl. In a separate bowl, whisk together the eggs, soured cream, sweetcorn and spring onions. Pour this into the dry ingredients, season and mix until blended. The batter should be fairly firm.

Grill the bacon until really crisp.

Heat 2 tablespoons oil in a frying pan over medium heat. Drop 2 tablespoons of batter into the pan and cook in batches of about 3, depending on the size of the pan. Cook the corn cakes for 2 minutes on each side, until golden brown and cooked through. Transfer to a plate and cover with foil to keep warm while you cook the rest.

Serve the corn cakes with a few slices of avocado, the crisp bacon and a couple of rocket leaves. Grind over some black pepper.

Crab cakes with slaw & sweet chilli sauce

500 g cooked crabmeat
50 g dried breadcrumbs
1 egg, beaten
3 tablespoons mayonnaise
¼ teaspoon cayenne pepper
3 tablespoons chopped
    fresh coriander leaves
4 tablespoons olive oil
sea salt and freshly ground
    black pepper
sweet chilli sauce, to serve

SLAW
1 apple, peeled
2 carrots
½ small red cabbage
6 spring onions, sliced
freshly squeezed juice
    of 1 lime
4 tablespoons mayonnaise
1 garlic clove, crushed
SERVES 4

Crab cakes are not cheap to make so it's a good choice when you have people coming over for more of a fancy lunchy brunch. Tinned crabmeat or a dressed crab will work, but if you do use dressed crab, omit the extra mayonnaise as it usually has some mayo already mixed in.

Put the crabmeat, breadcrumbs, egg, mayonnaise, cayenne pepper and coriander in a large mixing bowl, season and mix until blended. Shape the mixture into 8 x 8-cm patties and lay on a sheet of greaseproof paper on a baking tray. Chill in the fridge for 1 hour.

Preheat the oven to low.

To make the slaw, feed the apple and carrots through the grater on your food processor, or do it by hand if you don't have one. Shred the cabbage by hand as thinly as you can, or use the slicing attachment on the food processor. Tip everything into a large bowl. Add the spring onions, lime juice, mayonnaise and garlic and stir well. Set aside while you finish the crab cakes.

Heat the oil in a large frying pan over high heat. Fry the crab cakes in batches (keeping them warm in the oven as you go) for 3–4 minutes on each side, until crisp and deep golden.

Spoon a mound of slaw onto each plate and serve 2 crab cakes on top. Serve with sweet chilli sauce.

Corn cakes with bacon & avocado (right)

Hot smoked salmon hash with dill crème fraîche

500 g new potatoes, halved

4 tablespoons olive oil

2 onions, sliced

150 g streaky bacon,
chopped

15 g butter

2 teaspoons capers

200 g hot smoked salmon,
broken into large chunks

150 g crème fraîche

freshly squeezed juice and
grated zest of 1 lime

1 tablespoon chopped
fresh dill

sea salt and freshly ground
black pepper

SERVES 4

Unlike the regular smoked salmon we know so well, hot smoked salmon looks cooked and flakes into beautiful chunks. Mixing it with streaky bacon works really well as they share the same smokiness. A dollop of crème fraîche infused with lime and dill adds a bit of well-needed freshness too.

Put a saucepan of water over medium heat and bring to the boil. Add a pinch of salt and the potatoes. Reduce the heat and leave it to simmer for 12–15 minutes, until the potatoes are tender.

Meanwhile, put half the oil, the onions and bacon in a frying pan. Cover with a lid and cook over low heat for 8–10 minutes, stirring occasionally, until softening. Remove the lid, turn up the heat slightly and cook for 3–4 minutes until slightly golden. Tip onto a plate and set aside.

Drain the potatoes and add the butter and remaining oil to the frying pan you just used for the onion mixture. Add the potatoes and cook over high heat for 5–6 minutes, until browning on all sides. Stir in the onion mixture, capers and salmon and cook for 3–4 minutes, until everything is sizzling and hot, then season.

Mix the crème fraîche, lime zest and enough juice to make it limey but not too runny. Stir in the dill and season. Serve the hash with a dollop of the crème fraîche.

Sweet potato, chorizo & fried egg hash

3 sweet potatoes,
peeled and cubed

2 red onions, peeled and
cut into wedges

1 red chilli, sliced

1 teaspoon cumin seeds

4 tablespoons extra virgin
olive oil

150 g chorizo, sliced

200 g cherry tomatoes,
halved

4 eggs

a handful of fresh flat-leaf
parsley leaves, chopped

sea salt and freshly ground
black pepper

SERVES 4

This is full of sweet, smoky flavours. I adore vibrant orange sweet potatoes for their unusual starchy taste and I find that anything containing chorizo quickly becomes a firm favourite in our home. Add a fried egg and you can't go wrong!

Preheat the oven to 180°C (350°F) Gas 4.

Put the potatoes, onions, chilli, cumin seeds and half the oil in a roasting tray and toss well. Roast in the preheated oven for 15 minutes. Remove the tray from the oven, throw in the chorizo and tomatoes and return to the oven for 20 minutes, until everything is tender and slightly charred.

Heat the remaining oil in a frying pan over high heat, then crack an egg in each corner and turn the heat right down. Cook for 2–3 minutes until the white has set. If you need to firm up the white, cover with the lid for 30 seconds.

Season the hash and stir in the parsley. Serve each portion of hash with a fried egg on top.

Hot smoked salmon hash with dill crème fraîche (left)

Dukkah & harissa sausage rolls

500 g minced lamb

1 teaspoon smoked
   paprika

1 teaspoon ground
   cinnamon

4 tablespoons harissa or
   sun-dried tomato paste

500 g ready-made
   puff pastry

1 egg, beaten

sea salt and freshly ground
   black pepper

DUKKAH

2 tablespoons sesame
   seeds

2 tablespoons pine nuts

1 teaspoon coriander
   seeds

1 teaspoon cumin seeds

a baking tray, lightly oiled

SERVES 4

The plain old sausage roll gets a bit of an exotic make-over here. When I realized that most people like to drench their sausage rolls in tomato ketchup I thought, why not add some tomato to the meat. Hopefully this is enough to prevent my rolls from the ketchup fate. Not only have I used lamb, not pork, for the filling, but I have also spiced it with cinnamon and smoked paprika. And the top is speckled with an Egyptian spice blend called dukkah. This blend varies from recipe to recipe, so feel free to use up any remnants of nuts or seeds that you have.

Preheat the oven to 200°C (400°F) Gas 6.

To make the dukkah, put the sesame seeds, pine nuts, coriander seeds, cumin seeds and a pinch of salt in a mortar. Bash them with the pestle until crushed, but try to maintain a little texture so they are not pounded into a powder.

Put the lamb, paprika, cinnamon and harissa in a mixing bowl with some seasoning and mix with your hands, squelching it all together until thoroughly blended together.

Roll out the pastry on a lightly floured work surface until you have a rectangle 25 × 60 cm (and about 3 mm thick). Cut into 4, at 15-cm intervals. This will give you 4 rectangles, each 25 × 15 cm. Spoon about 4 tablespoons of the sausage mixture onto each rectangle. Brush a little beaten egg along one short side. Fold the pastry over from one short side to meet the other short side. Press the folded edges together to seal and crimp by pressing down with a fork. Leave the other 2 sides of the rolls open so that you can still see the filling.

Repeat to make 3 more rolls. Brush them with more beaten egg and sprinkle the dukkah over the top. Transfer to the prepared baking tray and bake in the preheated oven for 25–35 minutes, until golden and cooked through.

Smoked haddock kedgeree

50 g butter

2 onions, thinly sliced

4 eggs

1 teaspoon ground cumin

1 teaspoon ground
coriander

½ teaspoon ground
turmeric

175 g basmati rice

300 ml boiling water

400 g smoked haddock

freshly squeezed juice
of 1 lemon

a handful of fresh curly
parsley leaves, chopped

SERVES 4

Kedgeree is an old English dish left over from the Victorian days when, in a flurry of Anglo-Indian mania, it graced breakfast tables around the land. It developed from a simple Indian dish of rice and lentils called khichari.

Bring a small saucepan of water to the boil for the eggs. Meanwhile, melt the butter in a casserole dish over low heat, add the onions and stir to coat in the butter. Cook, covered, for 10 minutes, stirring occasionally, until soft. Put the eggs in the pan of boiling water and turn it down to a gentle simmer. Simmer for 8 minutes. Drain and run them under cold water. Take the lid off the onions, add the spices and turn up the heat. Cook, stirring, for 3–4 minutes, until the onions are golden brown. Add the rice, stir and pour in the 300 ml boiling water. Cover with the lid and turn the heat down so it gently simmers for 8 minutes.

Put the haddock in a frying pan and cover with boiling water. Simmer gently for 5–6 minutes, until cooked though, then drain. Turn off the heat under the rice, keep covered and leave to steam for 10 minutes. Peel and halve the eggs. Drain the fish and remove the skin and any bones. Flake into chunks and stir into the rice with the lemon juice and parsley. Serve topped with the boiled eggs.

Linguine with lemon, basil & parmesan cream

25 g butter

2 shallots, finely chopped

1 unwaxed lemon

300 ml whipping cream

200 ml hot chicken or
vegetable stock

2 handfuls of fresh basil
leaves, plus more to
serve

350 g dried linguine

75 g Parmesan or Pecorino
shavings, plus extra
to serve

sea salt and freshly ground
black pepper

SERVES 4

I'm not suggesting you have pasta for breakfast, but if your brunch is a late one, this is an easy dish to whip up. I sometimes add a splash of vodka to the shallots too, which just gives it a slight acidic edge, as wine does. Make sure you go for unwaxed lemons so you are not ingesting all the horrid chemicals on waxed ones.

Heat the butter in a frying pan and add the shallots. Add a pinch of salt, cover and cook over low heat for 6–7 minutes, stirring every now and then, until soft and glossy.

Put a large saucepan of water on to boil for the pasta. Meanwhile, take a potato peeler and pare off the zest of the lemon, leaving behind the white pith. Try to pare the zest in one long piece so you can easily remove it later.

Add the cream, stock, lemon zest and basil to the shallots and gently simmer for 10–15 minutes, uncovered, until it has reduced and thickened – it should only just coat the back of a spoon. Cook the linguine in the boiling water until al dente.

Season the sauce with a little salt and lots of pepper. Fish out the lemon zest. Drain the pasta and return to the pan. Stir in the Parmesan and squeeze in some juice from the lemon. Add more juice or seasoning, to taste. Garnish with more basil and Parmesan shavings.

Linguine with lemon, basil & parmesan cream (left)

sandwiches, salads & sides

Steak & fried egg baps with mustard butter Hot chorizo, avocado & lime sandwiches **Gravadlax with pickles on rye bread** Reubens with beef, sauerkraut & emmenthal Spiced omelette sandwiches with tomato & chilli jam **Quinoa salad with smoked chicken, avocado, pea shoots & toasted almonds** Red rice, dried cherry & pistachio salad with halloumi Pickled herring, beetroot, fennel & chicory salad with yoghurt dressing **Hash browns** Bacon & onion rösti Baked beans with maple syrup & paprika **Bacon rolls with chilli & pecan nuts** Roasted balsamic tomatoes

Steak & fried egg baps with mustard butter

100 g butter, softened

2 teaspoons wholegrain mustard

½ teaspoon English mustard powder

1 tablespoon chopped fresh tarragon leaves

1 teaspoon Gentleman's relish or anchovy paste (optional)

2 white baps, halved horizontally

2 x 250-g rib-eye or sirloin steaks, roughly 1.5 cm thick

3 tablespoons olive oil

2 large eggs

sea salt and freshly ground black pepper

SERVES 2

A well-cooked steak with a rosy interior and charred exterior truly is a wonderful thing. I like to adorn it with a butter spiked with the piquant flavour of mustard and tarragon. When the steak is ready, it is clamped in a soft white bap slathered in this delicious butter, which will melt with the steak's residual heat. Along with a fried egg cooked so it is only just runny inside, this is one sandwich that you need to eat fast before the egg and butter have time to trickle down your chin.

Put the butter in a mixing bowl and beat it with a spoon until squished against the sides of the bowl. Spoon in the wholegrain mustard, mustard powder, tarragon and relish, if using. Season to taste, taking care not to over-season as the relish will already be salty. Beat everything together and use to butter the insides of the baps.

Heat a ridged griddle pan over high heat until very hot. Brush the steaks with 1 tablespoon of the oil and season. Using tongs, lay the steaks on the griddle and press down. Leave them to cook for 2–4 minutes on each side. Press the centre of the steak to determine how well cooked it is. A light yield means it is medium, while anything soft is still rare. Transfer the steaks to a board and cut off any large pieces of fat. Leave to rest for 2–3 minutes while you cook the eggs.

Add the remaining oil to a frying pan and heat over high heat. Crack in the eggs and turn the heat to low. Cook for 2 minutes, then flip over for 30 seconds to cook the other side, but leave the yolk with a bit of ooze. Place a steak in each bap and finish off with a fried egg.

Hot chorizo, avocado & lime sandwiches

1 avocado

freshly squeezed juice of ½ lime

110 g chorizo, sliced diagonally

4 slices of pain de campagne

25 g rocket

sea salt and freshly ground black pepper

SERVES 2

A good nutty avocado is hard to beat. All it needs is some lime juice to perk up the natural flavours. Pair it with sweet, spicy chorizo and you instantly have the perfect sandwich.

Halve the avocado and remove the stone. Using a spoon, scoop out the flesh and mash in a bowl with the lime juice and some seasoning. Set aside.

Heat a frying pan over high heat, then add the chorizo. Fry for 1 minute on each side, or until crisp and lightly browned. Remove from the heat.

Toast the bread and spread the avocado over 2 slices. Top with the chorizo and a handful of rocket and sandwich with the other piece of toast.

Steak & fried egg baps with mustard butter (right)

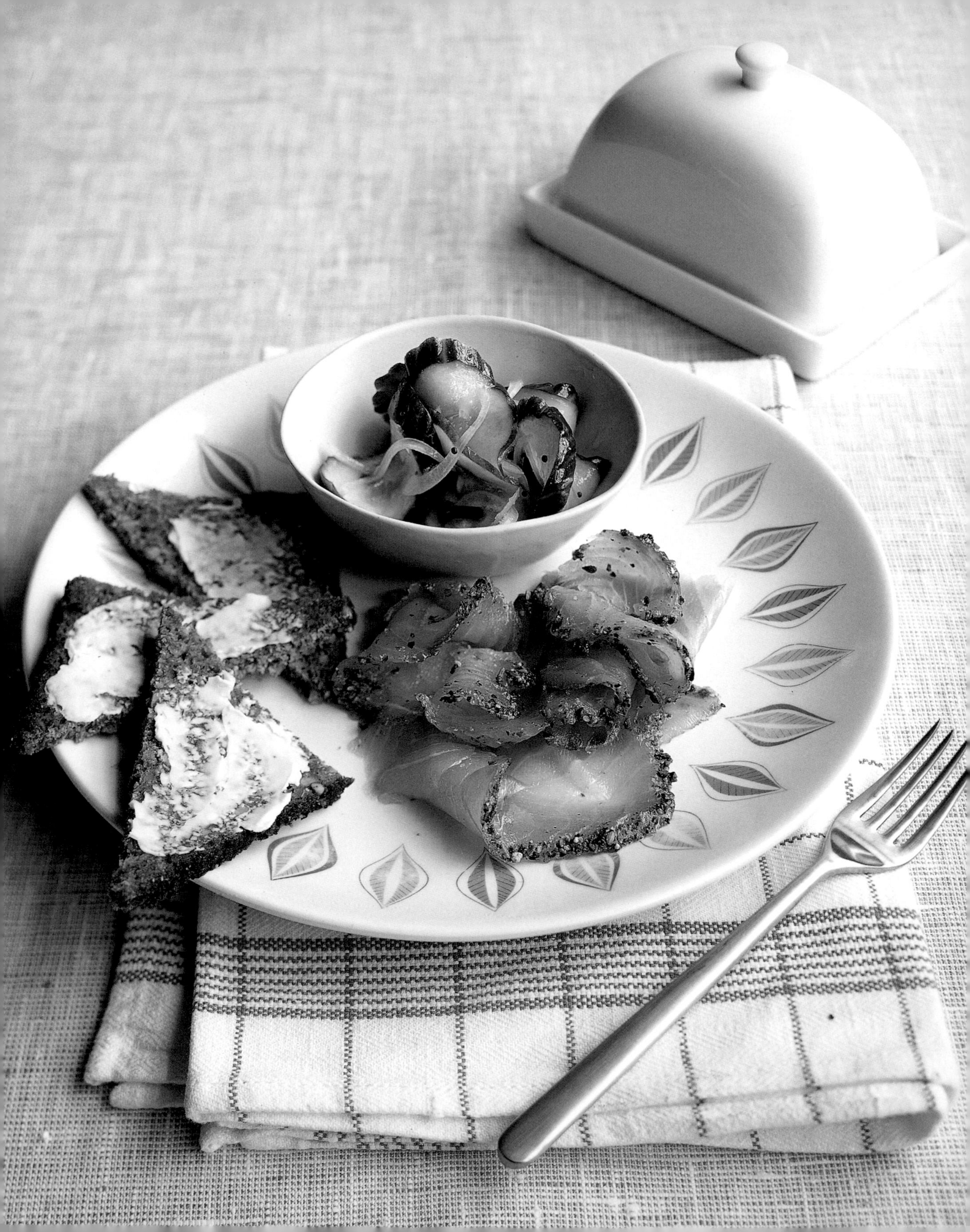

Gravadlax with pickles on rye bread

buttered dark rye bread,
   to serve

GRAVADLAX

1 tablespoon juniper
   berries
1 tablespoon fennel seeds
1 tablespoon black
   peppercorns
50 g coarse sea salt
4 tablespoons demerara
   sugar
750 g salmon fillet,
   2–3 cm thick, pin boned
   and scaled

PICKLES

2 cucumbers, sliced
   5 mm thick
1 small onion, thinly sliced
2 tablespoons sea salt
¼ teaspoon celery seeds
1 teaspoon mustard seeds
2 tablespoons prepared
   horseradish
5 whole cloves
250 ml white wine vinegar
200 g granulated sugar
SERVES 6–8

I like to make this for a brunch party as it feeds many unexpected guests without any extra effort. Making both the pickles and gravadlax is mainly an assault on your dry stores, so don't be put off by the lengthy list of ingredients. Refrigerated pickles will keep for up to 1 month, which is why the recipe makes a lot more than you can eat in one sitting. The gravadlax is very easy although it does need to be thought about a few days earlier, but once it is done you can forget about it. Make sure you start with the freshest fish as it is ultimately eaten cured but raw.

To make the pickles, put the cucumbers, onion and salt in a large non-metal bowl. Cover and chill in the fridge for 2 hours. Rinse and drain well. Transfer to a medium container. In a small saucepan, heat the celery seeds, mustard seeds, horseradish, cloves, vinegar and sugar. Bring to the boil, to dissolve the sugar, then pour onto the container with the cucumbers. Cover and refrigerate for 1 day to develop a full flavour.

To make the gravadlax, pound the juniper berries, fennel seeds, peppercorns, 1 tablespoon of the salt and the sugar with a pestle and mortar until roughly crushed and aromatic.

Line a non-metal tray with clingfilm, leaving enough overlapping to wrap around the salmon later. Scatter one-quarter of the ground spices over the clingfilm and lay the salmon, skin side down, on top. Cover with the rest of the ground spices. Wrap tightly in the clingfilm so you form a watertight parcel and weight down with tins of food or a heavy board. Leave to cure for 12 hours or overnight in the fridge. Flip the fish over, weight down again and cure for another 12 hours and continue to cure and flip until the fish has had 48 hours.

Unwrap the fish and drain off any juices. Place on a board, skin side down. Slice the gravadlax thinly with a sharp knife, cutting the flesh away from the skin (discard the skin). Serve with buttered rye bread and pickles.

Reubens with beef, sauerkraut & emmenthal

4 tablespoons mayonnaise

3 spring onions, sliced

2 gherkins, chopped

¼ teaspoon hot
horseradish sauce

a dash of Worcestershire
sauce

a pinch of caster sugar

8 slices of rye bread

300 g corned or salt beef,
sliced

200 g sauerkraut, drained

100 g Emmenthal, sliced

SERVES 4

This is a classic American sandwich which contains corned beef (or salt beef), thousand island dressing, sauerkraut and melted Swiss cheese. I am not a huge fan of the dressing so I have tweaked mine slightly.

Put the mayonnaise, spring onions, gherkins, horseradish and Worcestershire sauces and sugar in a bowl, mix well and set aside.

Preheat the grill.

Grill the bread for 1–2 minutes on one side, until golden. Remove from the oven and spread dressing over the untoasted side of half the slices. Lay the Emmenthal on the rest and grill for 2–3 minutes to melt.

Meanwhile, put the corned beef, then some sauerkraut over the mayonnaise-covered bread slices. Once the cheese has melted, make up the sandwiches and serve immediately.

Spiced omelette sandwiches with tomato & chilli jam

8 large eggs

1 teaspoon ground cumin

a small handful of fresh
coriander leaves, chopped

2 tablespoons olive oil

1 long baguette

80 g lamb's lettuce

sea salt and freshly ground
black pepper

TOMATO & CHILLI JAM

250 g tomatoes, chopped

2 large red chillies,
deseeded and chopped,
plus 1 just chopped

1 red onion, chopped

3 garlic cloves, sliced

1 cm fresh ginger, grated

4 tablespoons red wine
vinegar

250 g demerara sugar

2 tablespoons fish sauce

SERVES 4

The tomato & chilli jam for these sandwiches is made in the oven. Watch it doesn't get too sticky as it will set and harden more on cooling, a bit like jam does. It makes a jarful but you can use it up on other dishes, as it will keep for a month in the fridge. I like using the extra with grilled fish and a dollop of soured cream.

Preheat the oven to 200°C (400°F) Gas 6.

To make the tomato & chilli jam, put the tomatoes, chillies, onion, garlic, ginger, vinegar and sugar in a roasting tray. Season with fish sauce, stir to combine and roast in the preheated oven for 30–40 minutes, until the tomatoes and onion are well cooked and caramelized. The jam will still be runny but will thicken as it cools. Leave to cool slightly.

Beat together the eggs, cumin and coriander and season. Heat a frying pan (about 20 cm in diameter), add the oil and swirl to coat the base of the pan.

Pour in half the egg mixture and draw the cooked edges into the centre. Tilt the pan so the uncooked egg runs into the edges. When the omelette is evenly set except for a little unset egg, it is done. Fold it in half and slide it out of the pan onto a board. Cook the remaining egg mixture in the same way.

Slice the baguette horizontally. Slice each omelette in half and stuff into the baguette. Smear with tomato & chilli jam (lots if everyone likes the heat) and add a tangle of lamb's lettuce. Cut the baguette into 4 portions and serve.

Reubens with beef, sauerkraut & emmenthal (right)

Quinoa salad with smoked chicken, avocado, pea shoots & toasted almonds

250 g quinoa

75 g shelled Marcona almonds, chopped

6 tablespoons extra virgin olive oil

3 tablespoons sherry vinegar

1 garlic clove, crushed

300 g smoked chicken, chopped

2 avocados, stoned and chopped

150 g cherry tomatoes, halved

50 g pea shoots

sea salt and freshly ground black pepper

SERVES 4

Quinoa is a grain with a very high protein content. It has a slightly frog spawn look about it, but it tastes like a nutty couscous or bulghur wheat. I adore pea shoots, which seem to be the ingredient *de rigueur*; they taste of peas but have the texture of a soft leaf. Along with smoky chicken and creamy avocado this makes a really gorgeous warm salad for a sunny mid-morning.

Soak the quinoa in a bowl of cold water for 20 minutes.

Meanwhile, put the almonds in a dry frying pan over medium heat and leave them to heat up. Stir so they brown evenly, then remove from the heat.

Bring a pan of 600 ml water to the boil and when the quinoa has had its time, drain and pour into the boiling water. Cook for 15 minutes.

Make a dressing by whisking together the oil, vinegar, garlic and some seasoning.

Put the chicken, avocados, tomatoes and toasted almonds in a large serving dish. When the quinoa is ready, drain it well and run it under cold water to stop it cooking. Drain again and tip into the dish with the vegetables. Add the dressing and toss together until blended. Gently fold in the pea shoots and serve.

Red rice, dried cherry & pistachio salad with halloumi

250 g Camargue red rice

100 g dried sour cherries

4 tablespoons extra virgin olive oil

1 tablespoon red wine vinegar

1 garlic clove, crushed

50 g shelled pistachios

6 spring onions, sliced

250 g halloumi, sliced

2 tablespoons chopped fresh mint leaves

4 tablespoons chopped fresh flat-leaf parsley leaves

sea salt and freshly ground black pepper

SERVES 4

The red rice from the Camargue region of France has a nutty texture. It needs a punchy dressing to wake it up so I have added a crushed garlic clove to a regular vinaigrette. Look out for dried sour cherries for this vibrant salad, but you can use dried cranberries or sultanas as a fallback.

Bring a medium saucepan of water to the boil and add the rice. Add a pinch of salt and simmer for 25–30 minutes, until the rice is tender but still has a bite to it.

Meanwhile, soak the cherries in 100 ml warm water, until they become really plump.

Make a dressing by whisking together 3 tablespoons of the oil, the vinegar and garlic and some seasoning. Drain the cherries and put in a large serving dish with the pistachios and spring onions.

Heat a ridged griddle pan over high heat. Brush the halloumi with the remaining oil and griddle for 1–2 minutes on each side, until branded with deep golden lines.

Drain the rice very well and add to the ingredients in the serving dish. Add the dressing and herbs and toss everything together until blended. Spoon onto plates and top with the halloumi.

Red rice, dried cherry & pistachio salad with halloumi (left)

Pickled herring, beetroot, fennel & chicory salad with yoghurt dressing

3–4 tablespoons olive oil
freshly squeezed juice
  of 1 lemon
1 fennel, trimmed and
  thinly sliced
sprig of fresh dill, chopped
250 g cooked or raw baby
  beetroot
100 g Greek yoghurt
1 tablespoon red wine
  vinegar
2 heads of chicory, sliced
280 g pickled herring, cubed
sea salt and freshly ground
  black pepper

SERVES 4

Pickled herring, or roll mops as they are sometimes known, are great in the morning as they are zingy and sweet. Mixed with slivers of fennel and a few bitter chicory leaves, they make for a very refined salad.

Mix together 3 tablespoons of the oil and the lemon juice, then put half of it into a large mixing bowl with the fennel and dill. Season well, toss together and set aside for 1 hour to soften the fennel. If you need to cook your beetroot, preheat the oven to 200°C (400°F) Gas 6.

To cook the beetroot, scrub it, then put in a small roasting tray with the remaining oil and some seasoning.

Cover with aluminium foil and roast in the preheated oven for 25–30 minutes, until tender. Cut this, or your pre-cooked beetroot, into quarters.

Stir the yoghurt and vinegar into the remaining oil and lemon juice dressing until well blended. Season to taste.

Add the chicory to the fennel in the bowl. Top with the beetroot and herring and serve with the yoghurt dressing.

Hash browns

25 g butter

1 onion, chopped

600 g large potatoes,
  peeled and grated

1 egg white, beaten

vegetable oil,
  for deep-frying

sea salt and freshly ground
  black pepper

MAKES 16

These hash browns are deep fried, which means you probably won't be making them every day, but like chips, it's great to sometimes make your own. If you need to keep them warm while you cook the rest of your breakfast, pop them in the oven but put them on a wire rack first so they don't go soggy.

Heat the butter in a frying pan, then add the onion, cover with a lid and cook over low heat until soft.

Put the potatoes into a large mixing bowl and stir in the softened onions. Stir in the egg white and season generously.

Fill a large saucepan one-third full with vegetable oil. Heat to 190°C (or until a blob of the potato mixture browns within a few seconds).

Roll the potato mixture into walnut-sized balls, then flatten slightly before adding to the hot oil. Fry in batches of 4–5 for 2–3 minutes, until golden brown. Drain on kitchen paper and serve with extra salt, for sprinkling.

Bacon & onion rösti

30 g unsalted butter

1 onion, sliced

75 g smoked bacon lardons

2 tablespoons chopped
   fresh sage leaves

650 g Desiree potatoes,
   peeled and grated

sea salt and freshly ground
   black pepper

a 20-cm non-stick frying pan

SERVES 4

There is something very comforting about lovely crispy rösti. It makes a good side dish to grilled sausages too.

Melt half the butter in the frying pan over low heat. Add the onion and bacon, raise the heat to medium and cook for 7–8 minutes, until soft and lightly browned. Stir in the sage, then tip into a mixing bowl with the potatoes.

Add the remaining butter to the pan. When it stops foaming, spread the potato mixture over the base of the pan and press down with the back of a spatula. Fry for 6–7 minutes without moving it. When it's golden underneath, flip it over and cook for the same amount on the other side too.

Baked beans with maple syrup & paprika

2 x 400-g tins haricot
  or pinto beans,
  or 400 g dried beans
25 g butter
250 g streaky bacon
  or pancetta
2 onions, chopped
1 teaspoon smoked
  paprika
2 teaspoons Dijon mustard
1 tablespoon tomato purée
250 ml hot stock
6 tablespoons maple syrup
sea salt and freshly ground
  black pepper
SERVES 4

These home-made baked beans are utterly delicious. They are sweet and smoky and so moreish. I like them piled on toasted and buttered granary bread, or served with some hash browns if I am feeling really naughty.

If using dried beans, put them in large bowl. Add enough water to cover by 8 cm and leave to stand overnight. The next day, drain the beans and put them in a saucepan of water. Bring to the boil and simmer for 40 minutes until tender. Drain.

Preheat the oven to 150°C (300°F) Gas 2.

Heat the butter in a large ovenproof casserole and fry the bacon until it has browned. Add the onions, paprika and mustard. Reduce the heat to low, cover with a lid and cook for 5 minutes, stirring occasionally, until it smells irresistible.

Add the cooked or tinned beans, tomato purée, stock and some seasoning. Cover with a lid and bake in the preheated oven for 2 hours.

Give everything a good stir, add the maple syrup and taste to check the seasoning. Bake for a further 20 minutes with the lid off until the sauce has thickened. Serve with hot buttered toast or Hash Browns (see page 126).

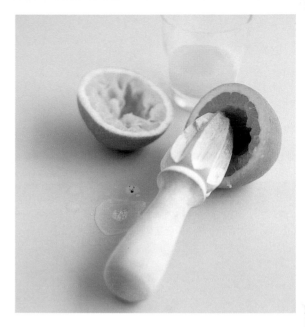

Bacon rolls with chilli & pecan nuts

¼–½ teaspoon hot
  chilli powder
2 tablespoons demerara
  sugar
25 g shelled pecan nuts
250 g streaky bacon
MAKES 16

These little rolls make a great change to regular crispy fried bacon. They are sweet but also have a fiery kick and a crisp texture from the chopped nuts.

Preheat the oven to 200°C (400°F) Gas 6. Put the chilli powder, sugar and pecan nuts in a food processor and briefly blend until chopped but still coarse. Lay the rashers of bacon on a baking tray and scatter a little of the ground mixture over them. Roll up each rasher and scatter a little more of the ground mixture over the top of each roll. Bake in the preheated oven for 15 minutes, until crisp.

Roasted balsamic tomatoes

6 plum tomatoes
2 teaspoons caster sugar
sprig of fresh thyme,
  leaves only
2 tablespoons olive oil
2 tablespoons balsamic
  vinegar
sea salt and freshly ground
  black pepper
SERVES 4

Roasted tomatoes make a lovely change from fried tomatoes. They go really well with Hash Browns (see page 126) or the Bacon Rolls above, but you could just as easily eat them cold in salads.

Preheat the oven to 150°C (300°F) Gas 2. Slice the plum tomatoes in half lengthways and arrange, cut side up, on a baking tray. Scatter over the sugar, thyme, oil and vinegar and season. Roast in the preheated oven for 1 hour, until they have lost some of their juiciness. Turn off the oven. Leave them to cool in the oven if there is time (to concentrate the flavours even further) or serve hot.

Bacon rolls with chilli & pecan nuts, and Roasted balsamic tomatoes (left)

preserves

Peanut butter Plum kernel jam **Rhubarb & ginger jam** Passion fruit curd Grapefruit & cardamom marmalade **Strawberry jam** White chocolate praline spread

Peanut butter

300 g shelled natural
    peanuts
2 teaspoons sea salt
5 tablespoons groundnut
    oil
2 tablespoons clear honey
1 or 2 large baking trays
2 x 200-ml jam jars,
    sterilized (see page 4)
MAKES 2 X 200-ML JARS

Why I've never thought about making my own peanut butter mystifies me. It is so easy and so much better than the shop-bought variety. You can make it with cashew nuts and almonds too, which would make fabulous gifts.

Preheat the oven to 180°C (350°F) Gas 4.

Put the peanuts, salt and 1 tablespoon of the oil in a large freezer bag and seal. Toss until the nuts are well coated. Tip out onto large baking trays, making sure the nuts are in a single layer. Roast in the preheated oven for 6–8 minutes, until lightly golden. Stir halfway through. Remove from the oven and leave to cool.

Put the nuts in a food processor and blend until roughly chopped. Remove a third of the nuts now if you want crunchy peanut butter. Add the honey to the remaining paste, scrape down the edges of the bowl with a spatula and blend again. Trickle in the remaining oil and keep blending until you have a very smooth, spreadable paste. Fold in the reserved chopped nuts. Transfer to the sterilized jars and use within 3 weeks.

Plum kernel jam

750 g (about 11) plums,
    halved
750 g preserving or
    granulated sugar
300 ml boiling water
freshly squeezed juice
    of ½ lemon
10 g unsalted butter
4 x 325-ml jam jars,
    sterilized (see page 4)
waxed paper discs,
    to fit your jam jars
MAKES 4 X 325-ML JARS

The kernels hidden inside plum stones give off an ambrosial aroma. I am lucky enough to have a plum tree in my garden so I have become very adept at this jam.

Remove the stones from the plums. Pop the stones in a freezer bag and whack with a rolling pin until the stones break and release the kernel. You only need 6 kernels, so discard the rest. Put the plums and sugar in a large, non-metal bowl, cover and leave overnight.

The next day, pop 2 or 3 saucers in the fridge. Put the reserved plum kernels in a large preserving pan or non-aluminium saucepan with the boiling water and lemon juice and bring back to the boil. Add the plums and sugar and cook for 20 minutes, or until they collapse. Squash them with the back of a spoon to help break up any large pieces, if necessary.

Raise the heat and boil for about 20–25 minutes, or until setting point has been reached – a sugar thermometer should read 105°C (220°F). To test for set, put ½ teaspoon of the jam on a chilled saucer, return it to the fridge or freezer for about 30 seconds or until cold, then prod the top. If a skin has formed, the jam is set. If not, return to the heat to cook for a little longer.

Stir in the butter to disperse any scum. Leave to cool for about 20 minutes, then transfer to the sterilized jars (wiping off any drips). Cover with waxed discs and seal with the lids whilst still warm. Label with the date and store in a cool, dark place for up to 6 months.

Peanut butter and Plum kernel jam (right)

Rhubarb & ginger jam

750 g rhubarb, trimmed
750 g granulated sugar
freshly squeezed juice
    of 2 lemons
5 cm fresh ginger, bruised
1 vanilla pod, halved
    lengthways
3 x 300-ml jam jars,
    sterilized (see page 4)
waxed paper discs,
    to fit your jam jars

MAKES 3 X 300-ML JARS

Rhubarb has that unique slightly metallic tang to it that you either love or loathe. I happen to love it and adore a jam made from it. Ginger and rhubarb have a natural affinity, but the vanilla helps to soften the flavours.

Chop the rhubarb into 5-cm lengths and drop into a non-metal bowl with the sugar. Cover and leave overnight.

The next day, pop 2 or 3 saucers in the fridge.

Transfer the rhubarb mixture to a large preserving pan or non-aluminium saucepan with the lemon juice and ginger. Scrape the seeds out of the vanilla pod and add to the pan along with the pod halves. Bring to the boil, then cook over low heat until the sugar has dissolved.

Raise the heat and boil for about 15–30 minutes – the timing will depend on whether you are using delicate forced rhubarb or tougher green rhubarb – or until setting point has been reached. A sugar thermometer should read 105°C (220°F). To test for set, put ½ teaspoon of the jam on a chilled saucer, return it to the fridge or freezer for about 30 seconds or until cold, then prod the top. If a skin has formed, the jam is set. If not, return to the heat to cook for a little longer.

Leave to cool for about 10 minutes, then fish out the ginger and vanilla pod and discard. Transfer to the sterilized jars (wiping off any drips). Cover with waxed discs and seal with the lids whilst still warm. Label with the date and store in a cool, dark place for up to 6 months.

Passion fruit curd

If you're a fan of lemon curd, then you will adore this. It is a little more perfumed than its lemony relative and somewhat sweeter. It goes brilliantly on any kind of bread or scone.

150 ml passion fruit pulp
  (from about 6 fruit)
freshly squeezed juice
  of 1 lemon
3 whole eggs
3 egg yolks
100 g golden caster sugar
100 g unsalted butter,
  chilled and cubed
*2 x 250-ml jam jars,
  sterilized (see page 4)*
*waxed paper discs,
  to fit your jam jars*
MAKES 2 X 250-ML JARS

Bring a saucepan of water to the boil.

Take a heatproof bowl that will sit over your pan of boiling water. Sieve the passion fruit pulp into the bowl and add the lemon juice, all the eggs and the sugar. Whisk until well mixed and set the bowl over the top of the pan of boiling water. Reduce the heat to low. Continue to whisk the mixture every 30 seconds, until it thickens. This should take about 10–15 minutes. Turn the heat off and add the cubed butter, whisking it in until the curd thickens.

Remove from the heat and continue to whisk until the mixture has cooled down. Transfer to the sterilized jars. Label with the date and keep refrigerated for up to 2 weeks.

Grapefruit & cardamom marmalade

2 grapefruits

4 lemons

about 900 g preserving
    sugar, or more

12 cardamom pods,
    crushed and seeds
    reserved

30-cm square of muslin

5 x 350-ml jam jars,
    sterilized (see page 4)

waxed paper discs,
    to fit your jam jars

MAKES 5 X 350-ML JARS

This is a very practical, easy way of making marmalade. The nonsense with muslin bags is simplified to make your life easier. The only thing you want to remember is you need to start the process a day early to give it time to extract the pectin. I love the tang of cardamom, which adds an unexpected level of flavour, but leave it out if you prefer.

Wash the grapefruits. Finely grate the zest, then wrap it up well with clingfilm and set aside until you need it the next day.

Halve the lemons and squeeze the juice into a large non-metal bowl, adding the pips. Halve the naked grapefruits and squeeze the juice into the bowl, discarding the pips. Chop up the lemon and grapefruit shells and add to the bowl with 2 litres water. Cover with a clean tea towel and leave in a cool place overnight.

The next day, pop 2 or 3 saucers in the fridge. Put the contents of the bowl into a large preserving pan or non-aluminium saucepan and bring to the boil over medium heat. Cover with a lid, then leave to simmer for about 1 hour.

Remove from the heat and leave to cool slightly. Line a sieve with your square of muslin and set the sieve over a large bowl. Pour the mixture through to strain out the solids. Press down on the cooked fruit shells to extract as much juice as possible, then discard them. Measure the juice (you should have about 1.25 litres), then weigh out the correct amount of sugar: there should be a ratio of 450 g sugar to 500 ml juice.

Pour the juice back into the pan and bring to the boil. Add the weighed sugar, cardamom seeds and grapefruit zest and boil for 20–25 minutes, or until setting point has been reached – a sugar thermometer should read 105°C (220°F). To test for set, put ½ teaspoon of the jam on a chilled saucer, return it to the fridge or freezer for about 30 seconds or until cold, then prod the top. If a skin has formed, the jam is set. If not, return to the heat to cook for a little longer.

Leave to cool for about 20 minutes, then transfer to the sterilized jars (wiping off any drips). Cover with waxed discs and seal with the lids whilst still warm. Label with the date and store in a cool, dark place for up to 6 months.

Strawberry jam

900 g slightly under-ripe
strawberries, hulled
and halved
750 g preserving or
granulated sugar
freshly squeezed juice
of 1 lemon
10 g butter
2 x 325-ml jam jars,
sterilized (see page 4)
waxed paper discs,
to fit your jam jars
MAKES 2 X 325-ML JARS

Macerating strawberries in sugar overnight reduces the amount of cooking time, which in turn means that the strawberries aren't cooked to mush, but retain some of their texture. You have to really watch for the setting point rather than relying on timing, as strawberries vary in water content and the more watery they are, the more cooking they will need.

Put the strawberries and sugar in a large non-metal bowl. Cover and leave to macerate overnight.

The next day, pop 2 or 3 saucers in the fridge. Transfer the contents of the bowl to a large preserving pan or non-aluminium saucepan and set over very low heat to dissolve any remaining sugar. Add the lemon juice and bring to the boil. Cook for 8–25 minutes, depending on the water content of the strawberries, or until setting point has been reached – a sugar thermometer should read 105°C (220°F).

To test for set, put ½ teaspoon of the jam on a chilled saucer, return it to the fridge or freezer for about 30 seconds or until cold, then prod the top. If a skin has formed, the jam is set. If not, return to the heat to cook for a little longer.

Stir in the butter to disperse any scum. Leave to cool for about 20 minutes, then transfer to the sterilized jars (wiping off any drips). Cover with waxed discs and seal with the lids whilst still warm. Label with the date and store in a cool, dark place for up to 6 months.

White chocolate praline spread

50 g shelled almonds,
chopped
200 g white chocolate,
chopped
300 ml double cream
2 x 250-ml jam jars,
sterilized (see page 4)
MAKES 2 X 250-ML JARS

This is so naughty, but it is great for special occasions. I stole the idea from a Belgian café where they had this on the table for children. My feeling was that adults should share in this joy too. The chocolate mixture is just like making truffles, except when you spread it on hot toast, it melts into every pore.

Put the almonds in a dry frying pan over medium heat and leave them to heat up. Stir so they brown evenly, then remove from the heat.

Put the chocolate and cream in a heatproof bowl over a saucepan of gently simmering water. Do not let the base of the bowl touch the water and keep the heat low because white chocolate has a

tendency to split. Leave to melt for 5 minutes. Remove from the heat and stir until smooth. Add the toasted almonds and fold through.

Remove the bowl from on top of the pan and leave to cool completely. Transfer to the sterilized jars and refrigerate for up to 1 week. Bring to room temperature before eating.

Strawberry jam (left)

index

author's acknowledgements

A heartfelt thanks to the whole team at Ryland Peters & Small: to Céline for her eagle eye and Megan for her creative eye, as well as Alison for giving me this project in the first place. It has been a lifetime in the making, as breakfast has always been my favourite part of the day. Thanks to my wonderful, ever-reliable assistant Vorney for ploughing through all the recipes with me in my kitchen and then again on the shoot. To Jonathan and Liz, what can I say? Your collaboration on this project has created the most beautiful breakfast and brunch book I have ever set eyes on. You are amazing! And lastly but by no means least, huge gushes of love to my husband and family who encourage and inspire me every day.